Cleveland Way

Dalesman Publishing Company
Stable Courtyard, Broughton Hall,
Skipton, North Yorkshire BD23 3AE

First Edition 1997

Text © Martin Collins 1997
Maps by Martin Collins
Cover photograph: East Coast from the
Cleveland Way by C R Kilvington

Printed by Amadeus Press, Huddersfield

A British Library Cataloguing in Publication
record is available for this book

ISBN 185568 113 7

Cleveland Way

Martin Collins

Series editor Terry Marsh

DALESMAN

The Cleveland Way

HARTLEPOOL

SALTBURN

MIDDLESBROUGH

GUISBOROUGH

WHITBY

OSMOTHERLEY

SCARBOROUGH

NORTHALLERTON

THIRSK

HELMSLEY

PICKERING

FILEY

BRIDLINGTON

Contents

Introduction

As far back as the 1930s when the freedom-to-roam banner was already being enthusiastically carried by thousands of city dwellers keen to enjoy the great outdoors, seeds were sown for a long-distance moors and coast path in North Yorkshire. It was to be provided with some of the recently-introduced youth hostels and would offer splendid holiday rambling within easy reach of industrial conurbations in the north of England.

By the time the North York Moors had become a National Park in 1952, the route was still far from being open to the public, although it had been given official approval by the then National Parks Commission (now the Countryside Commission). A further 16 years elapsed before the complexities of access agreements and path preparation were complete. The Cleveland Way was finally opened at Helmsley Youth Hostel on May 24, 1969.

The trail sweeps in a great arc from the market town of Helmsley round the Hambleton and Cleveland Hills escarpments to the North Sea at Saltburn, thereafter following cliff paths south to Filey. Such an extraordinary contrast, between on the one hand farmland, woods and heather moorland (some of the most extensive and beautiful in England), and on the other hand a dramatic stretch of Heritage Coast, is unique among Britain's National Trails. Indeed, scenic variety and magnificent views have become hallmarks of the Cleveland Way.

The underlying geology along most of the trail is composed of sedimentary rocks, such as sandstones and shale, laid down in oceans and river deltas during the Jurassic period, over 150 million years ago. They happen to be particularly rich in fossils, especially ammonites, which are depicted in Whitby's town crest.

Initially the trail traverses a limestone plateau where the flat-topped Tabular Hills that border the Vale of York merge with the Hambleton Hills. At Sutton Bank, arable farmland suddenly gives way to a dramatic escarpment overlooking the vales of York and Mowbray with views ranging to the distant Pennines.

Turning east at Osmotherley, the Cleveland Hills escarpment is followed on a switchback of moor-land summits revealing beneath the vegetation the ochres and pinks of Ravenscar sandstones. There is a brief flirtation with the main moorland block at its highest point on Urra Moor before a continuation of the Cleveland Hills descends gradually to the North Sea at Saltburn.

Already ravaged by erosion over several million years, the coast is currently retreating at an average rate of 2in (5cm) a year. During the Great Ice Age, extensive layers of glacial clays and sands were plastered over solid rocks and these remain un-stable, constantly slumping as waves undercut the cliff base. Promontories and headlands of more resistant strata, and wave-cut platforms locally called scars extending out at beach level, all bear testimony to nature's ceaseless battleground at the margin between land and sea. Inland too, ice, rain and wind all play their part in shaping the landscape, as they have done over aeons of time.

All along the trail there are constant reminders of how man has occupied and exploited the land since prehistoric times, among them Iron Age hillforts, Bronze Age burial mounds, ancient trackways. Roman signal stations down the coast warned of Saxon invaders, and following the Norman Conquest in 1066 great abbeys and castles were built, their present-day ruins a source of fascination and awe. You will encounter many associations with Captain Cook, explorer of new lands in the 18th century, and with other things maritime from smuggling, whaling and fishing to shipwrecks, for which the coast has always been notorious.

But it is the old quarrying and mining industries that have left the most conspicuous legacies, both in the hillsides and along the cliffs. Jet, a form of fossilised wood, was collected from the seashore and fashioned into jewellery by Bronze Age man some 4,000 years ago. Commercial mining and artefact production reached its zenith at Whitby in the late 19th century.

Between the 17th and 19th centuries, alum shale played a central role in textile dyeing and tanning. Usually found close to deposits of jet, it was extracted in vast quantities, often completely transforming local landscapes and leaving behind great quarries and pink-hued slag hills which now have been largely recolonised by undergrowth. Graphic examples are found at Carlton Bank on the Cleveland Hills escarpment and at Boulby, Sandsend and Ravenscar on the coast.

During the mid-1800s Britain's appetite for iron became insatiable. Mines small and large were opened to meet this demand wherever ironstone seams could be located. By far the richest deposits were around Rosedale and an audacious high-level railway line was constructed to transport the ore over the moors, down a cable-operated incline to Battersby Junction and thence to the smelting mills of Teesside and Durham. Part of the old railway trackbed is followed by the Cleveland Way.

Limestone and sandstone have long been quarried in the region for building, and whinstone for road construction. More recently, potash salt contained in 200 million-year-old rocks from the Permian Age is being extracted at Boulby for agricultural applications. Up to 4,000ft (1,220m) below ground level, these workings are the deepest in Britain.

Whilst historical sites and industrial archaeology provide points of interest for Cleveland Wayfarers, the walking itself leads through a succession of natural environments (though it is as well to bear in mind that today's English landscape owes as much to the evolution of farming techniques through the ages as it does to nature. By the end of the Middle Ages, for example, man's profligate harvesting of timber, foraging by livestock and climate changes had already decimated the great forests of birch and pine that once clothed the moors).

Except for arable crops growing on the limestone

Hambleton Hills, farming in the dales and plains adjacent to the hills is mostly concerned with cattle, pigs and poultry. Widespread across the moors, hardy black-faced Swaledale sheep share their rugged habitat with red grouse which are shot in the name of sport for four months each autumn. For the benefit of both species the heather is carefully managed by periodic burning back to encourage the growth of tender young shoots. In late summer these vast moorlands are illuminated by a glorious purple haze as heather and ling come into flower, a magnificent sight. Other upland birds you can expect to encounter along the trail include curlew, lapwing, golden plover and meadow pipit.

The Cleveland Way passes through several woods, some broad-leaved, but many of pine, larch and spruce belonging to the Forestry Commission.

On the coastal section from Saltburn south to Filey, clifftops often form the fringe of cultivated land. Here as elsewhere around our shores the call and antics of seabirds form a memorable background to coastal walking: species include gulls, fulmars, redshanks, kittiwakes and cormorants, with rock pools and sandy shallows providing a feeding ground for waders. In many locations, sheltered wooded ravines and glens running inland contain rich flora and fauna above little inlets known locally as 'wykes'.

Whether on the escarpments, the moors or the coast, horizons are exhilaratingly wide yet there always seems to be an abundance of wayside detail to hold the attention: an orchid in a disused quarry, the hum of honey bees amongst the heather, sunlight on ancient masonry, or the hypnotic roar of surf.

The Cleveland Way Project

In an atmosphere of post-war optimism about peace and enjoyment of the great outdoors, 1949 saw the passing of the National Parks and Access to the Countryside Act. Under it the Countryside Commission was given the duty of identifying long-distance routes which would be suitable for walkers, horseriders and cyclists and which for the most part avoided roads. First to be approved was the Pennine Way, opened in 1965, followed four years later by the Cleveland Way.

Over the intervening years, many thousands of people have enjoyed what is now known as the Cleveland Way National Trail, both as a continuous long-distance trek and in segments incorporated into local walks. Our National Trails are meant to reflect the very highest standards of path management for they are truly the country's flagship routes. Not surprisingly then, considerable concern was expressed about serious erosion problems developing along parts of the trail after its first 20 years of use.

In 1988 a Cleveland Way Project Officer was appointed to research into the usage and condition of the trail and to produce a management strategy for the future. This strategy has been adopted as a guide in all management and marketing decisions by the Cleveland Way Project which itself is a partnership between the Countryside Commission, the North York Moors National Park and relevant local authorities.

Much work goes on behind the scenes dealing with issues such as reconciling the sometimes conflicting interests of walkers and farmers, undertaking conservation of natural habitats, improving the Cleveland Way's contribution to local economies, and so on. However, of more immediate interest to walkers will be the footpath renovation which has been continuing for a number of years. Some of the varied techniques involved include pitching (creating irregular stone steps and ramps on steeper gradients); consolidation using aggregate; and forming traditional flag paths from reclaimed paving slabs airlifted in. Once weathered down, these new moorland path constructions – not attempted since the days of packhorses – will prevent environmental damage and should last upwards of 100 years with only minor maintenance.

The Project team is also responsible for, among other things, waymarking and the upkeep of trail furniture such as stiles, gates and bridges; for helping to improve infrastructure (public transport, accommodation and information provision); and for continuing to monitor the trail's wear and tear as recreation along it increases in popularity.

Planning your walk

Officially the Cleveland Way's total length is 110 miles (177km), though precision is hard to achieve over such distances. Small twists and turns, wandering off the exact path line and exploring towns and villages will all result in a somewhat higher mileage, not to mention diverting off-route for refreshments, shopping and accommodation.

Most walkers of average ability take around 8 days to complete the trail, that's about 14 miles (22km) a day. If this seems too far (or not far enough!) stages can be adjusted accordingly. However, accommodation along the way is not uniformly available so careful planning is advisable. The following information and advice is intended to help ensure that your trip is a successful and trouble-free one.

Accommodation

This will determine the style of your journey, its cost and to some extent the weight you will need to carry in your rucksack. The Cleveland Way Project publishes an annually-updated accommodation and information booklet giving details of hotels, guest houses, campsites and youth hostels on or close to the trail. It also tells you where food is available. A local company, Cleveland Way Support Services, offers a door-to-door baggage transfer for walkers, including help with advance bookings. (See 'Useful Addresses').

Hotels and B&Bs: Widely used by walkers, though sometimes a couple of miles (3km) or more off-route. You are assured of a warm welcome, a hot shower or bath and sustaining food at the beginning and end of the day. Wet clothes and footwear can often be dried out, but you will need to carry a spare 'indoor' outfit. Specifications vary according to price and during the summer you will need to book ahead. One disadvantage of booking the entire trip in advance is having to keep up with your self-imposed timetable; adverse weather, injury or fatigue can all conspire to slow you down, taking the enjoyment out of reaching your destination. If arriving at a town without booked accommodation, the Tourist Information Centre will usually find you a bed for the night.

Youth Hostels and Camping: Despite their title, youth hostels these days offer low-cost accom-modation for all ages; some provide a meals service too. Hostels on the Cleveland Way are situated at: Helmsley (Tel. 01439 770433), Osmotherley (Tel. 01609 883575), Whitby (Tel. 01947 602878), Boggle Hole (Robin Hood's Bay) (Tel. 01947 880352) and Scarborough (Tel. 01723 361176).

In response to the wishes of walkers, bunkhouse accommodation and camping barns are becoming more prevalent. Facilities vary from basic to 'all mod cons' and allow for self-catering. Supplies may be available from the farm and sleeping bags may sometimes be hired but otherwise must be taken with you.

There are three kinds of camping pitch. Official campsites will usually possess showers, washing-up facilities and a shop. Better appointed ones may have washing and drying machines, perhaps a restaurant, and even a games room!

Many farms adjacent to the trail are happy to allow lightweight campers to pitch overnight on request (though preferably not large groups). You may get only water and somewhere to pitch your tent so you need to be self-sufficient. Farm produce such as eggs and milk is sometimes available.

Wild camping by experienced backpackers is feasible in some locations but not on open moorland within the National Park, nor in Forestry Commission woodland where there is serious risk of fire. Because the landscape is quite intensively used and settled compared to true wilderness country, finding sources of clean water can be problematic. Except in emergencies, permission to camp should always be sought before putting up a tent. Needless to say, litter should be carried away or burned and every care taken not to pollute the environment. The backpacker's code is to leave no trace of your stay.

Camping undoubtedly increases flexibility for overnight halts but it would be folly to set off carrying all the necessary gear without having first become accustomed to the extra pack weight involved and the techniques for camping successfully in all weathers.

NOTE: Should you wish to park a car in a public place while walking the Cleveland Way, please contact the nearest Tourist Information Centre, or alternatively the police, for advice.

Public Transport

Helmsley, the Cleveland Way's western terminus, can be reached by bus from the railway stations at Thirsk, Malton and York. If you plan to walk counter-clockwise, Filey, the eastern terminus, is on the rail network.

Since deregulation bus services have become fragmented, making it impossible to provide accurate, up-to-date information in a guidebook such as this. Happily, a guide called Moors Connections, available free from Tourist Information Centres, gives full details of all the bus and train services around the North York Moors region. By using this, public transport can often be used to get back to your starting point at the end of a linear walk, or to avoid the necessity of parking a car in a lonely and vulnerable location.

Walking conditions and weather

As in all upland regions of Britain, the best advice for walkers on the Cleveland Way is 'Go Prepared'. A potentially enormous range of walking conditions exists in this moorland area close to the inhospitable North Sea. Even in summer, while one walker is enjoying the dales or forest in relative comfort, his counterpart on the exposed tops could well be battling against low temperatures and driving rain.

Paths and tracks on the moors are predominantly stony, but along the coast and over farmland the going can be very slippery. Although steep slopes are encountered on the Cleveland Way, gradients are rarely sustained enough to represent danger like they do in true mountain country. The exception to this is the coastal section where high, slumping cliffs frequently carry away stretches of path in the more erosion-prone locations. Vigilance is needed wherever the trail threads along the cliff edge, particularly during and immediately after stormy weather. Walkers are also strongly advised to take account of tide times so as not to risk becoming stranded while beach walking. The sea shows no mercy to those making foolish or hasty decisions. Other hazards common to walking in general include exposure to the elements and plain exhaustion, both of which can normally be anticipated and guarded against.

Although the weather in North Yorkshire and Cleveland can be warm and sunny, more often than not it is moderated by winds blowing off the chilly North Sea. In average years June is the sunniest month and, along with March, the driest, while August, November and January are wettest. Rainfall, however, is appreciably less here than in most other parts of Britain.

Depending on weather patterns, snow cover may be expected on about 30 days a year, perhaps up to 45 days on the moortops where winter blizzards can produce severe walking conditions. When cold air arrives from the north-east, it often condenses to form the notorious roak, a dense sea fog rolling in to blanket the coast and moors and prompting walkers to reach for their map and compass!

It is prudent to obtain an up-to-date weather forecast before setting out. A 'Weathercall' 24-hour forecast for North East England is available by phoning (0891) 500 418.

Equipment, safety and supplies

Experienced walkers will have their own tried-and-tested outdoor gear and will readily be able to assess the day's walking requirements. Those newer to walking, however, may not feel so confident. The following notes are offered as advice appropriate to the Cleveland Way Trail.

Well-fitting, comfortable boots add immeasurably to the enjoyment of walking. Try out new boots before embarking on a long-distance trek; blisters and soreness tend to appear sooner when carrying a rucksack that is heavier than usual. Lightweight boots will be perfectly suitable, even trainers if you are blessed with a spell of settled summer weather.

What to wear depends to a large extent on the time of year, though as a general rule several thin layers are more versatile than one thick one. Garments made from modern durable synthetic fibres provide excellent insulation as well as wicking perspiration away from your skin – infinitely preferable to the cold clamminess of wet cotton! For the same reason jeans are best avoided, being uncomfortable when damp and slow drying.

Shell clothing (cagoule and overtrousers) are virtually indispensable for protection against wind and rain, a dangerous combination even in summer. The more expensive breathable garments double as windproofs without the condensation problems of cheaper pvc-coated nylon.

Winter expeditions on the higher stretches of the

Cleveland Way should always be treated seriously. Clothing, equipment (and the walker wearing them!) need to be able to withstand potentially hostile weather. Extras should include warm headgear, gloves, emergency rations such as chocolate and mintcake, adequate drinks, a torch and whistle, a plastic survival bag (or tent) and spare warm clothing. Winter or summer, carry a small first aid kit and, of course, map and compass. In hot summer sunshine cover up with lightweight, loose clothing and a brimmed sunhat and remember to carry plenty of liquid. At such times special care is needed to avoid starting a moorland or forest fire.

In the unhappy event of an accident, serious injury or illness, or the verified loss of a fellow walker, write down the map reference of your position and call the police by dialling 999. They will advise the best course of action and if necessary initiate a rescue.

To attract attention in an emergency make the International Distress Call, one long signal (whistle blast, torch flash or similar) every ten seconds for one minute. The answer is three signals per minute, but keep on signalling to guide rescuers towards you.

Probably the greatest danger is exposure due to a drastic fall in the victim's body temperature. Cold winds, driving rain (or snow) and wet clothing are the most common causes. Symptoms include slurred speech, uncharacteristic behaviour such as stumbling and loss of interest in what is happening, pallor and shivering. Insulate the casualty from the ground, get him/her as warm and dry as possible by whatever means, but don't administer alcoholic drinks or rub the skin. Sweet food such as chocolate can transform the situation, but in serious cases medical help is imperative. Exposure can kill!

Refreshment places such as pubs and cafes are never more than a few miles distant wherever you are on the Cleveland Way. That is no comfort, however, outside opening hours, during the low season or when fighting against a strong headwind. Common sense suggests that some sustaining food is carried.

Food and associated items can usually be purchased at Helmsley, Osmotherley, Kildale, Skelton, Saltburn, Staithes, Runswick Bay, Sandsend, Whitby, Robin Hood's Bay, Ravenscar, Scarborough and Filey. For details of other supplies, banks, post offices, buses etc., contact the nearest Tourist Information Centres. Equally helpful may be enquiries at pubs, farms and the like. Finally make sure you take enough cash with you: there are not many cash dispensers on the Cleveland Way!

Maps and waymarking

Waymarking along the trail takes two main forms: timber fingerposts and plaques bearing the carved words "Cleveland Way"; and the Countryside Commission's acorn symbol, which is used on all National Trails. In theory, waymarking should take all the guesswork out of navigation. In practice this may not always be the case. Waymarks themselves are vulnerable to vandalism, including removal or deliberate misalignment; they may become obscured by undergrowth, snow, heavy frost or even parked vehicles; and in mist they may be invisible unless you are close. It is therefore sensible to carry a map and compass (and know how to use them!) and to follow this guidebook's directions.

A map is essential should you wander off the trail and become lost, or simply need to detour off-route for any reason. The following sheets cover the Cleveland Way:-

OS Landranger 1:50,000 (1¼" to 1 mile, or 2cm to 1km) Sheets 93, 94, 99, 100 and 101.

OS Outdoor Leisure 1:25,000 (2½" to 1 mile, or 4cm to 1km) Sheets 26 and 27.

The final section from Scarborough to Filey is covered on OS Pathfinder 1:25,000 Sheet 624 (TA/08/09/18), which during the currency of this guidebook will be replaced with one of the new series of Explorer maps.

How to use this guide

Route details are given first for walkers travelling clockwise from Helmsley to Filey, the more usual way, but are also summarised in a separate section for walkers wishing to tackle the trail counter-clockwise from Filey to Helmsley.

The trail has been divided into three stages, each

possessing a distinctive character of its own and representing around two to four days' walking, depending on individual ability and accommodation preferences. (A useful chart of distances between places along the way can be found in the Cleveland Way Project's annually updated Accommodation and Information Guide).

1   Hambleton Hills

Setting off on any long-distance trail brings a surge of excitement and anticipation, but there is usually a period of adjustment for body and equipment. The Cleveland Way offers a leisurely initial stage ideal for such a shake down. Gentle field and woodland paths meander across the Hambleton Hills' dip slope to their sensational escarpment above the Vale of York. With few significant gradients, the trail then follows the scarp on ancient trackways before descending to Osmotherley at the threshold of the Cleveland Hills.

Helmsley, where most Cleveland Wayfarers begin, is a pretty Ryedale market town offering plenty of accommodation, shops and amenities. Nowadays, smart boutiques and antique shops rub shoulders with traditional stores and the town caters for a regular influx of visitors, especially during the summer. Yet whilst Helmsley has not been slow to exploit its own picturesqueness, beneath the veneer of tourism, rural small-town life continues much as it has for generations.

The North York Moors National Park Information Service has its headquarters in Bondgate, just along the Market Square with its two crosses, ancient and modern (market day is Friday).

The imposing memorial is to William, 2nd Lord Feversham, while along a path behind the Town Hall tourist information office stands Helmsley Castle. It was built around the turn of the 12th and 13th centuries by Robert de Roos, Lord of Helmsley. Many subsequent additions were made up to the 1600s though much of the oldest masonry has long since disappeared. Following a three month siege by a thousand Parliamentary troops during the Civil War, the castle was finally surrendered honourably on 22 November 1644. It eventually became a source of local building stone, a fate shared by so many other historic sites across the country. Nevertheless those sections standing are well preserved and the entire complex with its earthworks and unique D-shaped keep is hugely impressive.

Helmsley to Osmotherley

21.6 miles (34.7km)

From the old Market Cross the Cleveland Way begins by passing the church lychgate entrance and heads west along appropriately-named Cleveland Way. As you follow a walled farm track there are good retrospective views of Helmsley Castle above its manicured grassy banks. Pass a kissing gate, walk left down a field edge and follow the field headlands along above Blackdale Howl Wood.

Watch for a finger-post on the left directing you into the steep and overgrown little valley; at the far side you climb steps then pass the concrete foundations of a 1939-45 war Polish army camp. The way now crosses the access track to Griff Lodge with wide views to the left over Ryedale and

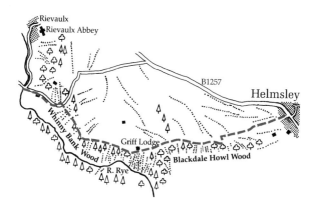

back to Duncombe House. The path hugs the top of Whinny Bank Wood then ambles easily down through Quarry Bank Wood to a bend in the Helmsley-Scawton road at Ingdale Howl. Turn left and in about 800m/yds you reach humpbacked Rievaulx Bridge; the 13th-century original was destroyed by flood in 1754.

If time allows, a detour to the right of just over 800m/yds each way along a riverside lane will take you to the magnificent ruins of Rievaulx Abbey.

Founded 850 years ago, the abbey's majestic architecture, right beside the River Rye, remains inspirational even today. From soaring walls, massive pillars and the symmetry of arch and window to close-range detail and texture, the ruins exude craftsmanship and harmony.

This was Northern England's first Cistercian monastery – according to St. Ailred in 1143: "a marvellous freedom from the tumult of the world". During its heyday the monastery was home to 140 choir monks and over 500 lay brothers (monks not in holy orders). The community thrived through sheep management, iron working, fish and salt production but towards the Dissolution of the Monasteries its fortunes had declined; by 1538 only 21 monks remained. After four centuries of religious life, self-sufficiency and enterprise the great abbey fell into disrepair and was ignominiously stripped for its building materials.

The Cleveland Way crosses Rievaulx Bridge, passing Ashberry Farm and the Old Byland road on the right. After about 900m/yds you turn right on to Bridge Road, a forestry track along by some small, secluded

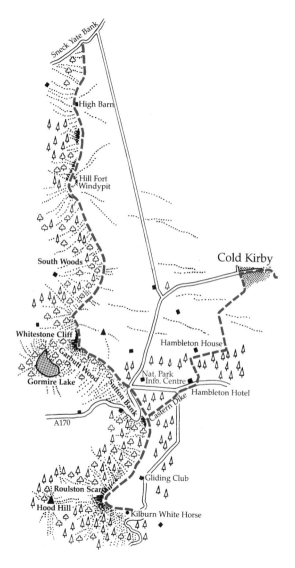

Sneck Yate Bank

High Barn

Hill Fort
Windypit

South Woods

Whitestone Cliff

Garbutt Wood

Gormire Lake

Sutton Bank

A170

Cold Kirby

Hambleton House

Nat. Park
Info. Centre

Hambleton Hotel

Casten Dike

Gliding Club

Roulston Scar

Hood Hill

Kilburn White Horse

31

Continue along the escarpment lip, swinging south then east from Roulston Scar, a great bastion of rock and a marvellous viewpoint. Below, fertile countryside stretches round from Kilburn village towards the Vales of Pickering and York and in good visibility you'll be able to make out the pale towers of York Minster 18 miles (29km) distant.

Directly opposite Roulston Scar stands pine-swathed Hood Hill, crowned by a crest of deciduous trees and Iron Age earthworks. Druid priests, it is said, held ritual sacrifices on its summit which is also associated with Robin Hood's final skirmish.

The easy path soon reaches the Kilburn White Horse, though from this angle it is barely recognisable. One of the best views of it can be gained from Carr Lane just north of Kilburn, and it is reputedly visible up to 70 miles (113km) away.

A Kilburn resident, one Thomas Taylor, initiated the White Horse project back in 1857 after seeing similar works in southern England. Local school children, supervised by their teacher, John Hodgson, marked out the design which was then cut by villagers. The whole thing measures 315ft (96m) long by 230ft (70m) high and occupies almost 2 acres. Because the underlying rock is grey limestone, not chalk like carved hill figures further south, it requires periodic dressings with Snowcem and chalk to maintain its whiteness.

You now retrace your steps back along the escarpment to Sutton Bank, passing en route the top of Thief's Highway, a steep path down the cliffside which developed as an escape route for highwaymen working the nearby Hambleton Drove Road. Beyond the end of Castern Dike a path bears left to a toposcope, or view table, pointing out such distant landmarks as Richmond in the Vale of Mowbray and Great Whernside, the latter 32 miles (52km) away.

There is a National Park Information Centre at Sutton Bank containing an informative exhibition about the area, a bookshop, café and toilets. A large car park betrays the enduring popularity of this delightful spot. Indeed, in 1802 those great celebrants of Britain's natural beauty, Dorothy and William Wordsworth, admired the vista on their way from Grasmere in the Lake District to visit William's wife-to-be at Brompton.

Cross over the main A170 near its junction with the Cold Kirby road, and continue along the escarpment. You soon pass a path forking down left towards Gormire Lake, part of the 2 mile (3.25km) Sutton Bank Nature Trail for which an booklet is available at the Information Centre.

Garbutt Wood is managed by the Yorkshire Wildlife Trust and contains such creatures as fox, badger, deer and squirrels. Gormire Lake itself, cradled in beautiful beech, ash and sycamore woodland and home to several waterfowl species, is reputedly bottomless, fed by underwater springs and with an overflow to the east which mysteriously disappears! The lake's enigmatic aura is buttressed by folklore and legend.

Before long the Cleveland Way turns a corner to confront the sheer, undercut Whitestone Cliff whose Upper Jurassic rocks date back 150 million years.

These formidable crags on the Hambleton Hills scarp were formed around 10,000 years ago when glacial ice, hundreds of feet thick extending between these moors and the Pennines, began to melt. Fast-flowing water from glacial lakes to the north took the line of least resistance along the ice edge next to the moor, scouring hillside channels and shaping the cliffs we see today. Gormire Lake was formed when a massive landslide blocked one such channel below Sutton Bank and Gormire Rigg. It is the North York Moors only natural lake.

A mile (1.6km) of pleasant walking alongside arable farmland above South Woods leads to Windypit Hill Fort, part of an Iron Age fortification on Boltby Scar. Thereafter the Way continues east of a wall above a disused quarry, through a gate and past High Barn, a wall to your right. Soon you bear left to a gate and follow the trail downhill to the road at Sneck Yate Bank.

Directly opposite, walk along a forest track on the now much less steep scarp; it passes above Low Paradise Farm and leads up to the access lane serving High Paradise Farm. This veers right, keeping left of the farm. Beyond a small plantation you reach the Hambleton Drove Road. In fact, further south several paths and tracks link the escarpment to the old drove road, but there it is tarmac. Here it remains in more authentic form, broad, rutted, predominantly grassy, and probably of prehistoric origin.

Many such drove roads and green lanes survive throughout Britain. Most were established in medieval times by the need to drive sheep and cattle to markets

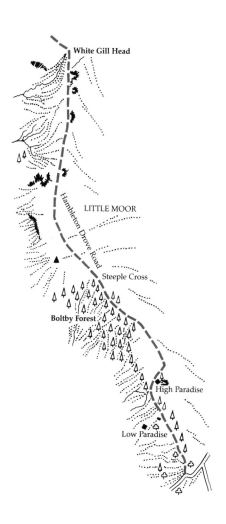

White Gill Head

LITTLE MOOR

Hambleton Drove Road

Steeple Cross

Boltby Forest

High Paradise

Low Paradise

serving expanding centres of population. Later during the Industrial Revolution, the demand for meat far exceeded the delivery capacity of rudimentary roads and an as-yet undeveloped railway system. Animals were driven south from as far afield as Scotland and the outer isles, grazing along the way and tended by a hardy breed of drovers who had to contend not only with bad weather and disease but also with attacks by thieves and confrontations with angry farmers on to whose land the stock inevitably strayed. Packhorses carrying lime, iron and other commodities also used these ancient thoroughfares which offered toll-free passage, even if the going was rough compared with the new turnpike roads then being built.

The line of the Hambleton Drove Road enters the North York Moors at Scarth Nick, climbing on to Osmotherley Moor and crossing Black Hambleton. After following the escarpment it descends to Oldstead and Coxwold and continues across the Vale of York. Happily it was never adopted as a motor road between Sneck Yate and the head of Oakdale, leaving this glorious stretch of high-level country to walkers, horseriders and the like.

The broad track heads north-west and from a gate makes a half mile (1km) foray through the edge of Boltby Forest before re-emerging on to open moor at Steeple Cross. The stone shaft, over to the right, bears the inscription CT 1770, referring to an estate boundary and the year of survey.

Flanked by a wall on the left, the Way crosses Little Moor, an open landscape of heather and grasses dotted with solitary trees. Cross the old road from

Kepwick to Hawnby and continue on through a gate into a walled section of drove road.

Just here once stood Limekiln House, a wayside inn at the centre of the lime-burning and distribution trade. The inn catered for thirsty drovers as well as quarrymen. There were other inns too beside the Hambleton Drove Road: Chequers, now a farm above Osmotherley; the Dialstone Inn north of Sutton Bank, now also a farmhouse; and the Hambleton Hotel passed earlier by the Cleveland Way – the only surviving hostelry.

In less than a mile (1.6km) of motorway width, the old grassy road forks sharply at White Gill Head. Keep left beside the substantial wall. The Way snakes along the flanks of Black Hambleton and there are extensive views over the wall to the west. Nearby Black Hambleton summit at 1,309ft (399m) represents the Hambleton Hills' northern limit.

Descending from a rough cairn, the track soon becomes deeply grooved in places due to erosion and the effects of rainwater run-off. If you can take your eyes off the ground, however, there are enticing views to the north taking in the Cleveland Plain and the Cleveland Hills' lumpy summits, with Osmotherley set on its natural shelf below the moors.

Further down, beyond the edge of moorside forestry, you cross a stretch of Thimbleby Moor to a car park and the Osmotherley-Hawnby road. To the north the drove road lies beneath Tarmac while the Cleveland Way swings left, on down the steepish, brackeny slopes of Thimbleby Moor into

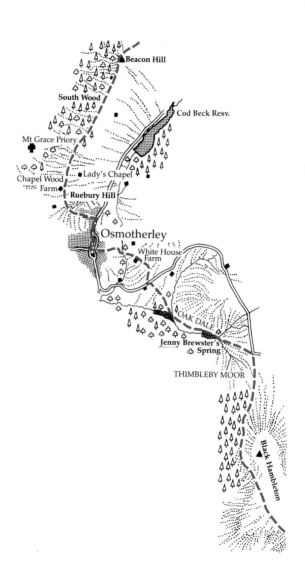

Beacon Hill

South Wood

Cod Beck Resv.

Mt Grace Priory

Chapel Wood
Farm

Lady's Chapel

Ruebury Hill

Osmotherley

White House
Farm

OAK DALE

Jenny Brewster's
Spring

THIMBLEBY MOOR

Black Hambleton

Oakdale. Here, Jenny Brewster's Gill babbles musically through a shady copse from where you walk along the right-hand shore of the upper of two diminutive reservoirs built a century ago: so unlike the vast flooded valleys of mid-Wales and the Pennines.

Below the dam and a ladder stile you pass former Oak Dale Farm, cross a bridge and climb from the wood ahead over a couple of fields to the same Osmotherley-Hawnby road encountered above. Cross over and take the next right turning, then a stile on the left, keeping to the right of White House Farm buildings. A footbridge spanning little Cod Beck is followed by steps up through a narrow wood. At the top bear left, cross two fields and Back Lane, where a short stretch of flag path takes you past the old Methodist chapel built in 1754 following a visit by John Wesley; it's one of England's earliest examples. And then through an archway, quite suddenly the route finds itself right in the centre of Osmotherley.

As the crow flies it is not far to Middlesbrough and industrial Teesside, nor to the constant rumble of traffic on the A19 trunk road, yet Osmotherley remains quintessentially rural in character. In a picturesque, flowery and rather self-conscious way it has managed to side-step the proliferation of tea rooms, gift shops and car parks to which so many pretty places submit. You either go there to enjoy its sleepy old-fashioned ambience or, as many do, you pass through en route for surrounding countryside.

Osmotherley was once an important market town with

darkened stone houses set at mid-level, aloof from both the Mowbray Plain and the high exposed moors to the east. The church contains fragments of Saxon crosses, 10th-century "hogsback" stones and a fine Norman doorway – testimony to a long history of settlement. At the village crossroads, where Cleveland Way walkers arrive, stands the ancient market cross. Nearby can be found a stone table upon which local produce was displayed for sale, and on which John Wesley stood while preaching to assembled villagers.

2 Cleveland Hills

With some 22 miles (35km) of quite gentle walking covered so far, somewhat sterner terrain lies ahead, though there is no lessening of scenic quality. The next section traverses the Cleveland Hills escarpment – a switchback of climbs and descents over high moorland. (A lower level alternative is also available in places). As you might expect, accommodation and refreshment points are also in less plentiful supply unless detours are made down to villages immediately beneath the escarpment.

Osmotherley to Saltburn-by-the-Sea

35 miles (56.3km)

The Way sets off north up the Swainby road past Bainbridge's General Store and turns left into residential Rueberry Lane. (Campsite and youth hostel are a little further up the road and off to the right). Rounding Rueberry Hill to Chapel Wood Farm an opportunity presents itself to visit Mount Grace Priory. However, due consideration should be given to the 400ft (122m) or so of descent and subsequent re-ascent involved. If the day's objective doesn't allow for such a detour, earmark it for another occasion.

Founded by Thomas de Holand, Duke of Surrey and Earl of Kent in 1398, Mount Grace was built up over the ensuing 40 years; it was Yorkshire's only Carthusian monastery. Monks lived here in silent solitude, but in considerably more comfort than we normally associate with monastic life. Each had his own cell comprising study, bedroom, workroom and small garden, water being piped in from hillside springs. Lay brothers apparently undertook the harder manual work, leaving the monks to their secluded life of books, gardening and prayer. Abandoned after the Dissolution of the Monasteries, the buildings were exposed to stone theft and erosion by the elements so that only the ground floor survives. Nevertheless, Mount Grace remains one of Britain's best examples of a Carthusian foundation, and is owned and cared for by the National Trust.

Almost opposite Chapel Wood Farm, an uphill path leads to Lady Chapel, attached to a stone house in a stand of pines. It was built around 1515, reputedly by Henry VIII's wife, Catherine of Aragon, as a Chapel of Ease for Mount Grace, and claims to have been the scene of several miracles.

The Cleveland Way continues as a cart-track into South Wood, open views replaced by mixed woodland. Higher up, in a birch clearing, sprouts an incongruous array of masts and aerial dishes belonging to a BT booster station. Long before the age of telecommunications fire beacons were lit hereabouts to warn of imminent attack or to celebrate special events.

Just over a wall to the right 200m/yds further on stands the trig pillar at the 981ft (299m) summit of Beacon Hill.

Historically, this was the start point for the Lyke Wake Walk, a 40 mile (64km), 24-hour challenge ending at the Raven Hall Hotel, Ravenscar on the North Sea coast between Whitby and Scarborough. Pioneered by Bill Cowley in 1955 as a tongue-in-cheek, old fashioned funeral wake, it soon grew in popularity to become the best known and most attempted long-distance tramp over the North York Moors.

Originally the route was largely undefined across vast expanses of heather moorland, but hundreds of thousands of feet (10,000 crossings were reported in a single year!) have produced alarming erosion. The National Park authorities are now requesting that only small parties attempt the walk, starting from Sheepwash

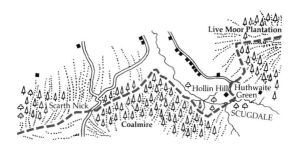

car park at the north end of Cod Beck Reservoir. Larger groups (e.g. charity fundraisers) should consider alternatives such as the Shepherds Round or the Hambleton Hobble.

Gates lead out on to a well-worn path across the open flanks of Scarth Wood Moor to the road at Scarth Nick, a notch in the escarpment created by glacial meltwater during the last Ice Age. Having turned a significant corner in the Cleveland Way, you are now heading north-east towards the coast at Saltburn and can look forward to some splendid moorland walking.

A waymarked gate near the cattle grid signals the onward route along a broad path through Coalmire plantation. After a while it loses height quite quickly and veers south-east into the pretty valley of Scugdale Beck on a wide, wooded path below Limekiln Bank; in years past this took all prizes for the deepest, stickiest mud, but has been tamed in recent times by deposits of aggregate!

In about 800m/yds a well-signed path leads down

over pasture to a ford and across the road bridge over Scugdale Beck. The Way then continues up past Hollin Hill Farm to the little crossroads at Huthwaite Green.

Ironstone mining on the flanks of Whorlton Moor and in Scugdale during the latter half of the 19th century has given way to forestry, an altogether more peaceful industry which, nonetheless, has transformed much of the northern escarpment. These dalesides were also worked for jet and alum, with old spoil heaps lining the 900ft (300m) contour like gargantuan molehills.

Huthwaite Green, the tiniest of hamlets on a back road south-east of Swainby, represents the beginning of true moorland for the Cleveland Wayfarer. However, over past decades here just as in other popular walking areas, countless thousands of booted feet bludgeoned footpaths into ugly scars and quagmires. Erosion was a serious problem: as well as the Cleveland Way and the Coast to Coast route, myriad circular, linear and challenge walks incorporate the Cleveland Hills escarpment, a recreational magnet for those living in nearby conurbations.

In response, extensive footpath renovation has been initiated by the Cleveland Way Project team, a partnership between the Countryside Commission, Redcar and Cleveland Borough Council, the North York Moors National Park Committee and Scarborough Borough Council. Techniques employed include pitching (creating irregular stone steps and ramps on steeper gradients); consolidation using aggregate; and forming traditional flag paths from reclaimed paving slabs airlifted in. Once weathered down, these new moorland path constructions – not previously attempted since the days of packhorses –

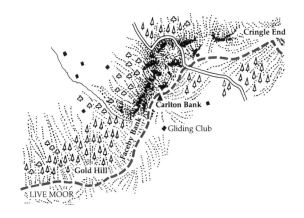

will prevent further environmental damage and should last upwards of 100 years with only minor maintenance.

To the right of a telephone kiosk the onward track climbs past overgrown mine spoil towards Live Moor Plantation, swinging left round the wood edge. Then, on your right, a long flight of steps climbs steeply up through trees on to Live Moor where the slope eventually eases off.

Boundary stones and bouldery outcrops of Ravenscar sandstone punctuate the otherwise featureless moortop but, like the Hambleton Hills already encountered, this scarp possesses its own special magic. Eyes will be drawn to Whorl Hill, now a mere kilometre away and dominating the foreground view, while away to the north-east, across the Cleveland Plain, Roseberry Topping rears its conical head.

Bearing to the south of Gold Hill (not as shown on the OS map), the restored path continues above Faceby Bank, leading straightforwardly up to the trig pillar and boundary stone at 1,338ft (408m) on Carlton Bank. On the way there you will have skirted the gliding club whose airfield occupies part of Carlton Moor summit.

Disused alum workings on the descent to the Bilsdale to Carlton-in-Cleveland road were ravaged over many years by motorcycle scrambling, no longer permitted there. Even so, on busy weekends this may not be a place in which to linger if you happen to be a walker for whom the hills are a source of quiet inspiration! Gliding, hang-gliding, kite flying and mountain biking are among the many activities practised in this accessible and popular location.

Across the road stands the Lord Stones Cafe, perhaps a welcome refreshment stop. Curving right over rough pasture you now tackle the ascent to the next summit on this big-dipper stretch, Cringle End. There you will find a stone bench, boundary marker and topograph, the latter dedicated to Alec Falconer, a local rambler and

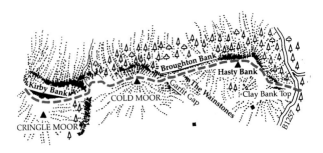

champion of walkers' interests who died in 1968, aged 84.

Below, as if seen from a low-flying aircraft, farmland spreads out towards the distant urban sprawl of Middlesbrough. Nearer to hand an old track circumvents the lower slopes of these hills from Cringle End to Clay Bank – a useful alternative in the event of bad weather, minor injury or such like.

The track was made by miners prospecting for jet during the 19th century, though finding deposits in the hillsides – usually narrow seams between alum rock and ironstone – was a hit or miss affair. The use of jet, a hard black variety of lignite (fossilised wood), to manufacture small articles dates back to the Bronze Age. Later, in the 8th century, the historian and ecclesiastical scholar Venerable Bede describes Britain as having, ".... Much and excellent jet which is black and sparkling, glittering at the fire and, when heated, drives away spirits...."

Certainly from the 14th century onwards crosses fashioned from jet were used as charms against witchcraft. But it was the demand for jet ornaments and jewellery, popularised by Queen Victoria and other worthy patrons, that made jet mining a tempting proposition, however speculative. Ultimately, cheaper Spanish imports and the substitution of imitation materials such as vulcanite and black wax sounded the industry's death knell around 1890. More will be heard of jet when the Cleveland Way reaches Whitby, one of the country's richest sources.

The Way now heads right in a bold concave sweep above the precipitous crags of Kirby Bank, some way north of Cringle Moor's true 1,417ft (432m) summit, at Drake Howe. A large depression, or col, separates Cringle Moor from Cold Moor, promising yet more legwork over bilberry and heather to attain this next dome of moorland.

Grouse are much in evidence, though the escarpment edge itself is not used for shooting. Birds frequently wait until the last moment before taking flight in a clatter of feathers and frantic squawks in front of a walker's footsteps – an alarming experience for both parties! Sheep and grouse both feed on the tender shoots of young heather which are encouraged by burning back mature plants each winter; patches of dense heather are left as shelter for grouse and their offspring, part of careful management which balances commercial interests against environmental considerations.

Entering a field on the right and following the clear, pitched path the route works its way upwards above afforested Broughton Bank and over the hump of Cold Moor at 1,317ft (401m) above sea level. The way forward is unequivocal, dropping through Garfit Gap then mounting towards Hasty Bank. As you gain height the path threads a miniature rock landscape, the Wainstones. These pinnacles and boulders form a popular playground for rock climbers, and even the walking route can involve an entertaining little scramble. Once through the rocks and out along the broad ridge of Hasty Bank, there are tremendous views ahead to Clay Bank Top.

Compared with preceding descents this next one is lengthier, involving a series of steps. Reaching the

B1257 Stokesley to Helmsley road, with camping opportunities and B&Bs within easy range, it's as well to take stock. No other human habitation or road is passed for the ensuing 6 miles (9.5km) to Battersby Moor and even then it is a further 2 miles (3km) to the tiny hamlet of Kildale with its post office/stores. Of course, this is not remote country in a true wilderness sense, but the steep, afforested escarpment prevents any easy escape should one become necessary. It is important, too, to bear in mind that moorland weather can deteriorate quickly and that in thick mist careful navigation on these exposed tops becomes imperative.

Directly across the road a gate leads into an uphill path over grassy hillside by a forest boundary wall; higher up it skirts left of a rocky channel before levelling off along the peaty crest of Carr Ridge.

To the south and east a much more expansive block of high moorland stretches to the horizon. A great feeling of freedom and openness lifts the spirits in such places yet, having temporarily left behind the drama of the escarpment, there is little of specific visual interest other than boundary stones and the occasional grouse. According to individual disposition you either concentrate on making rapid progress or allow the mind to wander on a higher plane! Before losing sight of it, glance back to the striking profile of Hasty Bank, surely the most impressive of the Cleveland Hills.

Urra Moor rises ahead and with it the track to Botton Head (or Round Hill) whose tumulus, crowned with a trig pillar, marks the highest ground in the entire North York Moors National

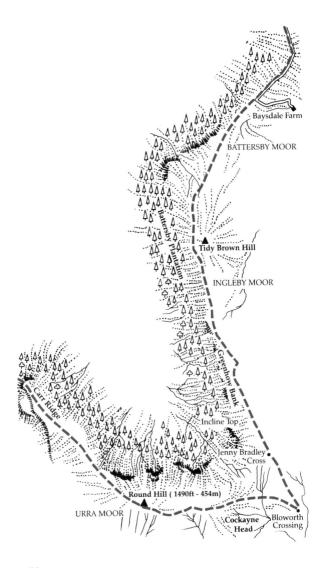

Baysdale Farm

BATTERSBY MOOR

Battersby Plantation

▲ Tidy Brown Hill

INGLEBY MOOR

Greenhow Bank

Carr Ridge

Incline Top

Jenny Bradley Cross

▲ Round Hill (1490ft - 454m)

URRA MOOR

Cockayne Head

Bloworth Crossing

Park at 1,490ft (454m) above sea level. A little farther on the eastbound track broadens to an astonishing 20ft (6m) or so in places, a section of old pannierway.

In the 17th century, trains of ponies equipped with various kinds of pannier slung on their backs transported commodities over this rough, inhospitable country between the coast and inland towns: coal and charcoal, wool and cloth, ironstone and lime. There can be little doubt that smuggled contraband, particularly illicit liquor, was also moved in this way! Without the network of hard surfaced causeways criss-crossing moor and dale, heavily-laden packhorses would soon have become bogged down in mud.

Two wayside stones mark your progress: the Hand Stone, a signpost almost three centuries old whose very badly eroded inscription refers to "Kirbie" (Kirkbymoorside) and "Stoxla" (Stokesley); and the Face Stone, probably even older and bearing a crudely-carved face on its eastern side.

From Cockayne Head, roughly 800m/yds beyond the Face Stone, the Cleveland Way continues east, dipping and trending right towards Bloworth Crossing.

During the 19th century, trains carrying iron-ore crossed the moors from mines around Rosedale and were lowered by cable down the escarpment at Ingleby Incline. From there they joined the main rail network to the smelting mills of Teesside and Durham. Bloworth Crossing, where the old coaching road along Rudland Rigg crossed the railway, was permanently manned by a level-crossing keeper, but the house is long gone. The old railway's cinder trackbed remains busy – not with trains, but with hikers on a number of well-established walking routes.

From Bloworth Crossing simply turn back sharp left (north-west) along the old, stony coaching road, soon encountering a moorland cross bearing the date 1888.

Before summer warmth has teased greenery from the earth, surrounding moor grasses are pale and tawny, their colour leached out by winter cold and a dearth of sunlight – a scene not without its own special charm. But walk from mid-August onwards and flowering heather and ling will have turned the landscape a glorious acid-purple. Whilst admiring the views, it is pertinent to remember that these heather moorlands are some of the most extensive in the whole of England.

It is easy going now on a stony swath along Greenhow Bank. From Tidy Brown Hill on Ingleby Moor you begin to lose height and within 1½ miles (2.5km) the narrow tarred road on Battersby Moor is reached. It ends at Baysdale Farm down to the east, but Cleveland Way interest lies ahead. Beyond a cattle grid it is downhill all the way and farewell to the escarpment for the time being.

Views west are as exhilarating as ever during the descent round beneath The Park, a spur of Kildale Moor, and finally the Esk Valley road is met. With some accommodation and a post office/stores, Kildale village, just along to the right, provides welcome respite from the lonely moors. It even has a railway station for the scenic Esk Valley line linking with the coast at Whitby.

Beyond the post office turn left towards the station, then almost immediately right, passing beneath the railway line and over the River Leven, a tributary of the Tees. The country road climbs to Bankside Farm, originally a traditional longhouse, in which farmer and livestock lived under the same roof. Above the farm buildings enter Pale End Plantation, being sure to turn sharp left (south-west and waymarked) at the top where a broad forest track continues through the larch trees. Not long after a left fork you emerge on to Easby Moor only 200m/yds or so from Captain Cook's Monument.

Robert Campion, a Whitby financier, erected the 51ft (15.5m) monument to Captain Cook in 1828, the centenary of his birth. The great circumnavigator's story is all there on cast-iron plaques, though the language is dated.

Born in 1728 at Marton on the outskirts of Middlesbrough, son of a Scottish farm labourer and his Yorkshire wife, James Cook attended school at Great Ayton after his family had moved to Airy Holme Farm in 1736. After a few years as farm hand, he left home to work as an apprentice draper in Staithes. He did not stay long! Already passionately interested in the sea, he served nine years in North Sea colliers before entering the Royal Navy at the age of 27. Progressing rapidly through the ranks, he joined expeditions to the then new lands of Canada and Newfoundland.

So great had Cook's reputation as a navigator become by

Highcliff Nab.

Highcliffe Farm

Hutton Lowcross Woods

Roseberry Topping

Slacks Wood

GT AYTON MOOR

Gribdale Gate

**Pale End
Plantation**

EASBY
MOOR

Capt.
Cook's Monument

Bankside Farm

River Leven

Kildale

The Park

the mid-1700s that he commanded surveys of New Zealand and the east Australian coast in HMS Endeavour, and went on to chart the South Pacific. On 14 February 1779, during a voyage to discover a new trading route to the East Indies, he was brutally murdered while rescuing members of his crew from natives at Kealakekua Bay, Hawaii, where the expedition had put in for supplies.

For devotees of the Captain Cook story there is a heritage centre at Staithes and more material at Whitby's Pannett Park Museum, both passed later on the Cleveland Way.

Despite being at 1,063ft (324m) above sea level – higher than nearby Roseberry Topping – there is little sense of standing on a summit on this largely wooded moortop. Heading north the Cleveland Way descends steps off Easby Moor then a broad, stony track between trees to a car park and picnic area at Gribdale Gate, the end of a lane rising from Great Ayton.

Now climb quite steeply on to the western lip of Great Ayton Moor, shadowing a wall on the left with wonderful views over the Cleveland Plain.

To the east, hut circles, cairns and ancient barrows, best seen after heather burning, provide visible links with our prehistoric ancestors who settled on this elevated land when the climate was much kinder than today's.

Swinging north-west above Slacks Wood the Way reaches a gate from which an out-and-back ascent of Roseberry Topping is made. The clear path drops to a shallow col then attacks the hill's steeper slopes. To laden backpackers it may seem unfair that the Cleveland Way demands this extra bit of legwork, but the climb is less than it appears: only 166ft (81m) compared with a beefier 750ft (215m) from the car park at Newton-under-Roseberry. From this angle it is hard to believe that the unseen west face is all crag and rock, a dangerous place in dense mist or strong winds.

Roseberry Topping is, indeed, a singular hill, a strange hybrid formed by a combination of natural forces and the hand of man. Ravaged by landslip and mining, its broken conical summit rears distinctively into views far and near, an anomalous shark's fin on otherwise rolling horizons.

Originally an island of rock protruding from a glacier's surface during the last Ice Age, (a "nunatak" or "rognon"), its geology is unstable and occasional rock falls continue to modify its profile. Until the 17th century, the hill was known as "Osbury Toppyne", and fire beacons lit upon its summit warned of the Spanish Armada and later of Charles Stuart's rebellious Jacobites. In more recent times, quarrying for jet, iron-ore and roadstone precipitated a major landslip in 1907, which sharpened the outline and gave rise to the epithet "the Yorkshire Matterhorn".

Situated as it is so close to population centres, this exciting landmark attracts all manner of visitors, not all of whom are bona fide walkers; graffiti on the trig pillar is a recurrent eyesore. Once acquired by the National Trust, an appeal was launched to finance much-needed work on paths, fencing, woodland management and bracken control, with obvious success.

Having bagged the 1,050ft (320m) summit, savoured the panorama and returned to the gate on Newton Moor, head east through heather to a gated corner of Hutton Lowcross Woods. The forest edge track leads along to the medieval Percy Cross Rigg road which runs across these moors from Guisborough Priory to Kirkbymoorside and is named after the powerful Percy family.

Turn right and in about 200m/yds head off left across the rough moorland of Black Nab, dropping through the little valley of The Race then along

outside the fields of Highcliffe Farm. Beyond the farm follow the steady uphill route and bear left through a gate beside Highcliff Wood. In 200m/yds turn up right, cross a forestry track and climb steeply to the right on to Highcliff Nab, well known locally for its rock-climbing crags. There are views too, both of Guisborough and, more enticingly, to Saltburn where the Cleveland Way meets the North Sea coast.

For the next 2½ miles (3.5km) through Guisborough Woods you will need to follow the map carefully. Take the eastbound scarp-edge forest road then in 800m/yds branch off left gently downhill. Bear right at the next junction, uphill at first then levelling off for nearly a mile (1,500m). Downhill from here walk along outside the forest, bearing right over a streambed and field to a stile. Turn left down a concrete road then right into a path between fences; at the end bear right through Spa Wood and uphill by the wood edge to a clearing. Heading east, eventually to cross a metal stile, turn left on to a descending track and left again along the old road at the bottom of the hill. This leads to the busy A171, adjacent to the Fox & Hounds pub – the first en-route hostelry for some 30 miles (48km). This descent to Slapewath, characterised by overgrown ironstone mine workings, represents a final descent from the Cleveland Hills themselves.

At the end of terraced houses where the old road sweeps left, take a path then a track up right, towards the quarry whose eastern rim is followed up steps through gorse. At the top a fenced path leads along above Rawcliffe Banks Wood to a stile. Here a field path then farm track goes past Airy Hill Farm. The access road (Airy Hill Lane) drops easily to Skelton Green, providing fine coastal views and taking walkers through the Cleveland Way's halfway point.

Refreshments and shops lie along to the right at

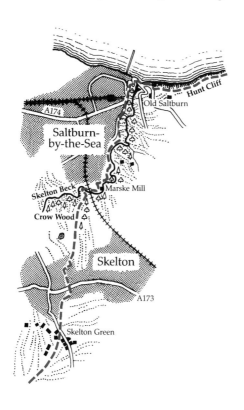

the main Boosbeck Road, but the Way enters a fenced tarmac path opposite, heading north through fields. When Skelton Castle is in view, turn right briefly along a lane at The Hills, then drop down steps on the left into Skelton. Cross the A173 and walk down Coniston Road for about 300m/yds, turning right into Ullswater Drive then left down Derwent Road.

The onward Way, possibly through further residential development in future years, continues downhill and enters Crow Wood where a twisting, stepped path goes down to Skelton Beck. A short distance downstream, cross the beck footbridge beneath the 783ft (240m) long railway viaduct over which trains laden with potash from Boulby Mine, near Staithes, occasionally rumble. Passing close to Marske Mill (the short stretch of path ahead forms part of the Marske Mill Heritage Trail), leave the woods and take an ascending track on the left. Saltburn town centre can be reached quickly along this lane.

The Cleveland Way, sights set firmly on the North Sea shoreline, bears right at a seat below a curving wall and continues down the wooded valley of Skelton Beck. Several attractive terraced paths thread down to the seafront, but the Cleveland Way climbs above Valley Gardens to join the main A174 road which jinks down across the beck's outlet at Saltburn Sands.

The rapid expansion of nearby Middlesbrough during the 19th and early 20th centuries was largely responsible for Saltburn's development from tiny fishing harbour to popular seaside resort. Henry Pease, an entrepreneurial Quaker businessman, was central to this change in Saltburn's fortunes for it was he who promoted an extension of the Stockton & Darlington railway line from Redcar to Marske and Saltburn.

In 1869-70 a 1,500ft (450m) long cast-iron pier was built for paddle-steamers, but the North Sea coast is an unforgiving location for such vulnerable structures. Badly damaged by a storm in 1875, it was cut in two when the "Ovenberg" collided with it and was wrecked during a gale in 1924. Although repaired, the pier suffered further storm damage, culminating in the destruction of all but the landward stump during a storm in 1970. In a way it symbolises Saltburn's wider demise. Changing patterns of holidaymaking, the increasing industrialisation and pollution of nearby Teesside and the insidious effects of recession and unemployment over recent decades have all contributed in their various ways to a steady decline in the town's prosperity. Yet the sands remain splendid by North Yorkshire standards, no less so than in the early part of the 20th century when motor racing speed trials were held here. If the winter scene is bleak, fine summer days see trippers and locals alike thronging the beach.

3 North Yorkshire and Cleveland Coast

Here and there a legacy of industrial activity stretching back over 100 years has left its mark on the margin between land and sea. Yet even without the scars of old alum, ironstone and jet workings, rampant marine erosion gnawing away at the great slipping faces of soft shales and boulder clay has sculpted a rugged cliffline notorious for shipwrecks and smuggling. Frequently assailed by bitter east winds and sea fog (known locally as 'roak') and pounded by a bullying North Sea, the Yorkshire and Cleveland coasts exude a kind of dour grandeur.

Fortunate indeed the walker who experiences blue skies, sunshine and balmy temperatures over this concluding section of the Cleveland Way. Not that you need fair weather to appreciate the historical and cultural gems with which this walk is studded. As well as a fascinating industrial heritage, there are fishing communities whose seafaring tradition reaches back many centuries, while two of the east coast's most popular holiday resorts – Whitby and Scarborough – are on the itinerary. From Saltburn to Scarborough is designated Heritage Coast.

Saltburn to Filey

53.4 miles (86km)

The Cleveland Way sets off south from behind the Ship Inn, a notorious smugglers' den, in the tiny village of Old Saltburn which until the mid-19th century comprised just sixteen houses. Colourful fishing cobles are often drawn up on the shingle bank, but the old path to seaward of the inn has long since disappeared. Steps take you up towards Hunt Cliff which rises to over 360ft (110m) above low tide rock scars. Inland, vast fields fill the skyline. Cobles, incidentally, are open boats unique to the east coast; built on Viking lines they are wide amidships with sharp bows to deal with the often heavy surf.

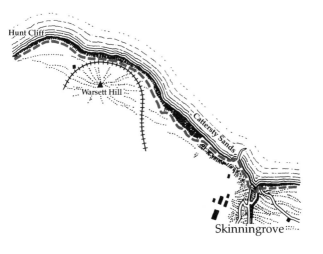

Hunt Cliff is the site of a Roman Signal Station, one of several down this coast built to warn of invaders and to summon reinforcements from York. Excavations in 1923 unearthed the incomplete skeletons of fourteen people thought to have been murdered by raiding Picts or Saxons during the Roman withdrawal from Britain.

For a short distance the path follows beside the railway track, then skirts pasture and fields before dropping to Skinningrove's Cattersty Sands over boot-clogging slag from the dismantled clifftop ironworks. Dunes and a jetty underpass lead into the village.

Skinningrove's old jetty has been comprehensively disembowelled by the sea. It still protects the little bay, caught between gaunt cliffs, but inconsequentially for today Skinningrove is an industrial ghost. Its ironstone seam was one of the first to be mined during the mid-1800s boom which was centred inland around Rosedale. So badly needed was an influx of new labour that in 1872 Skinningrove was developed as a then modern mining village of terraced dwellings.

It all seems strangely out of place today on this Heritage Coast, but we should remember that the iron industry offered relative wealth to local people whose only other source of income would have been farming or fishing, neither of which offered much more than subsistence living. Skinningrove grew because ore, coal and a moderately sheltered harbour on this inhospitable coast allowed profitable iron production to take place – at least until the early 20th century when higher quality imports and the effects of the General Strike heralded the industry's decline. For a more detailed appraisal of

Skinningrove's past, see the village's Tom Leonard Museum situated in the former Loftus ironstone mine.

From the car park walk left along Marine Terrace and round over the bridge spanning Kilton Beck, its waters permanently stained from iron-ore waste. Past a few fishing cobles and jumbled rows of pigeon lofts, the cliff path resumes, climbing steeply at first, then outside field boundaries above Hummersea Scar.

A century or more before ironstone exploitation, alum had been quite intensively mined and purified on the cliffs below. It was used as a fixing agent for textile dyes, to cure animal hides and to size paper. Alum was eventually superseded by a process mixing coal shales with sulphuric acid.

Soon after Snilah Pond the trail is waymarked inland, veering left past isolated Warren Cottage. Thereafter a stiled field path continues gently uphill to regain the clifftop where you re-enter the

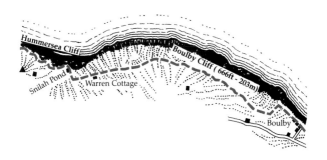

North York Moors National Park and reach Boulby Cliff. At 666ft (203m) it is the loftiest sea cliff on England's eastern seaboard.

These are not cliffs, however, in the mould of a Beachy Head or a Land's End whose steep rock faces plummet to the sea. Boulby's summit is less determinate, set back above sprawling undercliffs riddled with alum, jet and ironstone mining levels.

Descending in stages reminiscent of moorland, the onward path is exhilarating and provides wonderful views ahead of indented cliffs and a tableland of green fields. The sole eyesore is Boulby potash mine.

No one will deny the commercial value of developing the potash field here, but the environmental impact of this huge installation is a high price to pay. The mine shafts

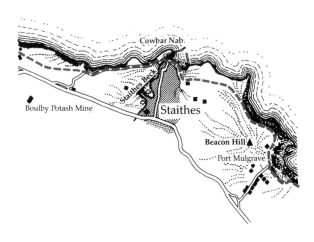

run out beneath the sea to a depth of over 4,000ft (1,220m), and the potash is used as an agricultural fertiliser. Although originally approved by the National Park Committee, future projects such as this may well be opposed.

Keeping seaward of dwellings at Boulby, built for workers at a nearby alum mine, the cliff path crosses fields to reach Cowbar Lane. During the steep descent into the glacial Staithes Beck gorge you can enjoy a classic panorama over Staithes' huddle of tall houses. You also pass from Redcar and Cleveland Borough into North Yorkshire.

The old village, protected from north-westerly gales by Cowbar Nab, has retained much of its original character. Fishing has always been its raison d'être, 300 locals having once been employed, the menfolk securing the catch at sea, the womenfolk gutting and repairing nets. After 1885, fish was crated out by rail to city markets, but eventually steam trawlers working from the larger ports monopolised catches, and the 120 or so cobles once based at Staithes gradually dwindled to the handful we see today. Crab and lobster fishing, however, perpetuates Staithes' long association with the sea.

Crossing the beck footbridge where the cobles are moored brings you to a short lane, at the top of which turn left down the cobbled street to Staithes' seafront.

Round above the little sandy beach by the Cod & Lobster Inn, its walls reinforced with steel after repeated damage by storm waves – notably in January 1953 – you gain a very real sense of the village's vulnerability, especially if a big sea is running. Houses have frequently been washed away in the past, but the construction of the breakwaters has afforded much improved protection.

On quieter days when the crush of tourists has gone it is easy to imagine that little has changed here since Captain Cook's day. As a lad in 1744, James Cook served his haberdashery apprenticeship in William Sanderson's shop, since rebuilt in Church Street. Eighteen months later, the sea well and truly in his blood, he began his illustrious career as a Royal Navy navigator and explorer of new lands. Staithes' Captain Cook Heritage Centre fills in the details and is well worth visiting.

Immediately beyond the Cod & Lobster turn right up Church Street past Captain Cook's cottage, climb steps and turn left up a sunken track on to the cliff path which levels off near modern farm buildings. Looking back it is clear how from this direction Staithes hides until you are almost upon it. Easy to follow, the Way crosses stiles through fields some distance back from the cliff edge, rising steeply over pasture on to the shoulder of Beacon Hill 378ft (115m), a fine viewpoint and site of an ancient signalling beacon.

At low tide the little bay of Brackenberry Wyke is seen to be paved with scars of Lias Limestone, a distinctive geological feature of this coast.

In no time at all the coast path leads to old coast-guard cottages above Port Mulgrave.

Far below, the diminutive harbour has become hopelessly choked with mud and stones; its jetty, ravaged by the sea, stands half-derelict. Yet this scene was once a hive of industry. Until Grinkle ironstone mines at nearby Dalehouse closed in 1916, ore had been transported from the workings by rope-hauled wagons through a mile-long tunnel (now sealed) and shipped out from Port Mulgrave to the furnaces of Jarrow.

Where the road to Hinderwell bends right at a sign for the Ship Inn, turn left and resume clifftop walking along the perimeter of arable fields. In rainy weather there is a little waterfall at Rosedale Wyke, while old fencing posts below the path around Lingrow Cliffs provide a graphic reminder, if one is needed, of this coastline's alarming instability. Indeed, one wild night in 1664 most of the original village of Runswick was swept into the sea on a massive landslip.

Being watchful to turn right at a stile, you will soon

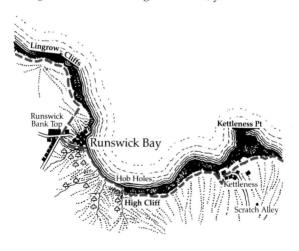

reach the Runswick Bay Hotel, turning left from the road junction along Bank Top Lane and taking the old road, now just a track sweeping downhill. On the left a stepped path descends past pretty cottages and flowery gardens to Runswick Bay village – better than taking the main road hill.

The community's fortunes hung on fishing in its early days and the industry's decline here mirrors that of neighbouring Staithes. Salvage from shipwrecks, the Kettleness alum quarries and Grinkle ironstone mines provided a little extra employment in what must often have been abrasively hard times. Little wonder that income was not always legitimately earned!

Runswick Bay, along with Staithes, was renowned as a smuggling centre during the 18th and early 19th centuries. Contraband included chocolate, tea, pepper, snuff and playing cards, as well as the more familiar spirits. It was brought ashore, secretly distributed inland and sold to the public by highly-organised teams of people. Despite the attempts of armed customs patrols, resulting in sometimes violent clashes, black market trade flourished until the government's conversion to the principles of free trade brought about a dramatic reduction in customs duties around the mid-1850s.

Real change at Runswick Bay was wrought by the arrival of the railway and the resulting inexorable shift towards catering for visitors. New houses were built above the bay, locals drifted away, shops closed through lack of regular customers and by the 1950s the holiday settlement we see today had become firmly established. Even so, many original buildings remain, renovated and prettified perhaps, but well worth taking time to admire.

There are steps down to Runswick Sands near rows of brightly coloured cobles hauled up by tractor on to hard standing by the car park. From here, except at the very highest tides, you can walk along the beach past the Sailing Club towards the cliffs of Kettleness Point.

Up to your right, concealed amongst trees and bushes, are the remains of holiday chalets, once fondly tended and connected by neat pathways, but now, like terrestrial "Marie Célestes", abandoned to subsidence.

Within 800m/yds, the Way approaches Hob Holes, natural caves enlarged by miners searching for jet during the 19th century, and since badly eroded by the sea.

Hobs, or goblins, appear in folklore and legends of the Yorkshire moors and dales; some were mischievous, others possessed curative or helpful dispositions. Runswick's hob was reputed to cure whooping cough, locally known as kink-cough.

Shortly beyond the caves, the Way turns up right into a stream valley, crosses a footbridge to the east bank and attacks the stiff 330ft (100m) stepped ascent on to High Cliff. Superb views back over the bay compensate for the legwork involved. The trail passes through Kettleness Farm near the cluster of redbrick houses built for railway employees before turning off left to the cliffline and soon encountering the old Loftus to Whitby railway trackbed.

Engineered with several tunnels and viaducts, this

supremely scenic line opened in 1883, linking Whitby to the existing Loftus-Middlesbrough line. Two years later a further section opened between Whitby and Scarborough, its trackbed approached by the Cleveland Way further down the coast.

About 800m/yds to the south-east, reached by lane and field path, rises the grassy mound of Scratch Alley,

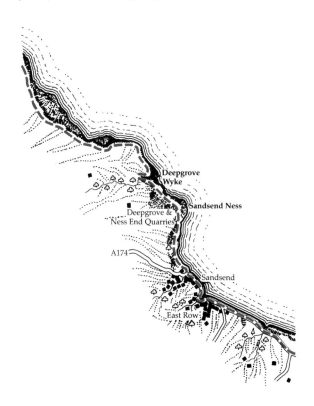

another Roman signal station. During its operational life in the 4th century, a timber or stone lookout tower would have stood atop the existing foundations.

Until it disappears into a sealed tunnel (constructed after the original line collapsed into the sea), the railway trackbed is closely shadowed by the coastal path, thereafter rising and dipping above slumped and eroded cliffs.

In fact, Kettleness, Keldowe and Sandsend Ness headlands were quarried and mined beyond recognition during the boom years of alum and jet production – testimony to the astonishing vigour of a largely unmechanised age. Whilst pondering such things, you may well glance ahead and notice the hilltop silhouette of Whitby Abbey ruin, now only some 4 miles (6.5km) distant as the seagull flies.

Once past Deepgrove Wyke where steep steps lead down to the second railway tunnel portal, walking regains the old trackbed snaking round towards Sandsend. Without the need to watch your footing, attention can be given to the overgrown alum quarries here at Deep Grove and Ness End, part of the 2-mile (3.2km) Sandsend Trail.

Wildlife has recolonised the quarry workings, waste tips and railway cutting. Birds frequenting the area include woodcock, snipe, sparrowhawk and green woodpecker; adjacent marshy hollows and woodland support many diverse plant and insect species. More details of wildlife and the alum industry itself are contained in a National Park booklet, The Sandsend Trail.

Descending flights of steps and bearing right across a car park brings you to the main A174 at Sandsend. If the tide is out, the preferred option is to beach-walk right along to Whitby, ending on the sea-level concrete "prom" lined with colourful beach huts. It is 2½ miles (4km) from Sandsend to West Pier. Should the tide be high, stay beside the road as it swings inland to the bridge over East Row Beck. About a mile (1.6km) east of Sandsend the road angles through Upgang Chine and along the back of the golf course.

"Chine" is a term normally associated with the south coast of England and the Isle of Wight. There it is commonly used to describe a stream-mouth ravine scoured out by the action of wind, rain and marine erosion.

Towards the far end of the golf course, take a track on the left opposite a caravan park. It ducks beneath a footbridge spanning another chine-like ravine before regaining the cliff path on the outskirts of Whitby. Continue downhill towards West Pier and follow the harbour inland beside the fish

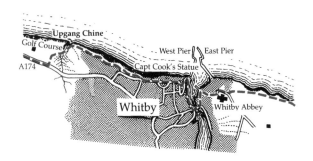

market to a swing bridge across the River Esk in the centre of town.

Despite a veneer of ice cream and candy floss, fish and chips and amusement arcades during the holiday season, Whitby retains its identity as a vigorous Yorkshire town and historic port here at the mouth of the River Esk. It is the largest and busiest town encountered thus far on the Cleveland Way and with so much to see it would be worthwhile setting aside a half-day or longer for exploration.

Facing each other across the harbour mouth are the Abbey ruins on East Cliff and the Captain Cook statue on West Cliff. Danes, Vikings and Henry VIII were all instrumental in the eventual destruction of Whitby Abbey, originally founded for both monks and nuns in 657AD by St. Hilda. It quickly became a centre for learning and the home of Caedmon, a talented poet mentioned by Bede and commemorated by a cross at the top of the 199 steps leading up to the Abbey known as Church Stairs. Shelled in 1914 during a German warship attack on a nearby coastguard station, the ruins we see today are largely 13th century.

Adjacent 12th-century St. Mary's Church is well worth visiting for its many fascinating interior details. The churchyard is associated with Bram Stoker's bloodthirsty vampire, Dracula, who purportedly arrived at Whitby in the guise of a large black dog!

For Cleveland Wayfarers journeying clockwise, Captain Cook will be no stranger, having passed his monument on Easby Moor and the scene of his early working life at Staithes. Cook's statue surveys the harbour, birthplace of "Endeavour", "Resolution", "Adventure" and "Discovery" that were to carry him around the world on his great exploratory expeditions.

Just below the statue a whalebone arch, presented by Norway, recalls Whitby's heyday as a whaling port during the late 18th and early 19th centuries. Whaling was always a hazardous occupation, but the financial rewards could be rich indeed. Whitby's most famous whaling captain, William Scoresby (inventor of the crow's nest), brought home over 500 whale carcasses – predominantly the Greenland right whale – during his career, a fifth of Whitby's total haul. Blubber was boiled and rendered on the quaysides to make oil for street lighting in the town as early as 1825.

Particularly from East Cliff there are wonderful views over the red-roofed cottages of Whitby's old quarter, a maze of narrow streets and alleyways above the harbour. These days they are lined with shops and restaurants catering for tourists, but the Whitby of old is portrayed in the atmospheric photographs of Frank Meadow Sutcliffe, who was born in Leeds in 1853, and came to Whitby as a young man. His work is featured in a town centre gallery.

A number of craft shops as well as the Pannet Park Museum contain innumerable examples of Whitby jet artefacts, many exquisitely fashioned. Essentially fossilised driftwood, 130 million years old, jet is a lightish, brown-black semi-precious stone which can be readily worked and will take a high polish. Whitby's famous jet industry began modestly enough in 1800, with around 50 workshops in production by 1850. However, when Queen Victoria endorsed jet as a symbol of mourning on the death of Albert, Prince Consort, in

1861, interest in jet jewellery burgeoned. Some 1,400 people were employed during the early 1870s, supplied by 200 miners locating deposits, but a mere decade later demand had dwindled with changing fashions and foreign imports.

Whitby's situation, surrounded on three sides by moorland and on the fourth by a stormy North Sea, is inescapably elemental, so that even if you walk through without pausing, its sights, sounds and smells will leave their mark on your memory.

Cross the swing bridge and turn left along Sandgate, or alternatively Church Street which leads along to the foot of the 14th-century Church Stairs. At the top (Whitby Plain), youth hostel and abbey will be on your right, while a path skirts St. Mary's churchyard to a car park. From here views over Whitby are spectacular. The Way now regains the clifftops on a popular, level stretch of path towards Saltwick Bay.

Ahead lies treacherous Saltwick Nab, scene of an heroic multiple lifeboat rescue when the troop hospital ship "Rohilla" ran aground in a gale en route for Dunkirk in October 1914.

Behind the promontory the trail bears right to approach Saltwick Bay Holiday Park, joining the surfaced road through the camping grounds and associated buildings. Beyond the shop a path descends left to the sands, but the Cleveland Way continues its clifftop course. Field edge stiles lead on to the foghorn, known locally as the "Hawsker Bull" or "T'awd Bull". Bearing half-right inland, the

Way passes behind the Whitby High Light 240ft (73m) above the waves. When operational it has a range of 22 miles (35km).

After climbing to a stile on the seaward edge of Ling Hill the path follows the undulations and ins and outs of the cliffline. In windy weather take extra care on exposed sections. Two small valleys – Oakham Beck, above Maw Wyke Hole, and Rain

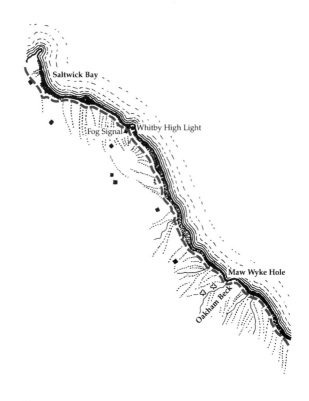

Dale – provide steeper gradients and potentially muddier going, but those apart the walk is straightforward and undemanding above cliffs of boulder clay falling precipitously to rocky scars.

As you swing round the curving thrust of Ness Point (or North Cheek) past an old coastguard lookout, Robin Hood's Bay comes into view. The coast sweeps ahead majestically towards Ravenscar as you draw near to Bay Town (the local name for Robin Hood's Bay village). A kissing gate and a short stretch lined with undergrowth bring you out on to a grassy track past houses.

Mount Pleasant North is an estate of houses originally built near the railway station for wealthy seamen and landowners during the village's heyday as a port.

Turning left along Station Road (B1447) will take you past the car park (only local traffic is allowed into the tortuous, narrow streets below) and down pedestrian steps towards the bottom of the hill and the most picturesque part of the village.

Despite its name, any connections with the famous outlaw of Sherwood Forest seem tenuous, particularly since Bay Town only became established well after the reign of Richard I. However, a legend does tell of Robin Hood helping the abbot of Whitby fend off Danish invaders. Since the 18th century, some 200 dwellings as well as the village's main road, King Street, have crumbled into the sea. Always rampant along this coastline of glacial clays, erosion has been checked by a massive sea wall 500ft (152m) long and 40ft (12m) high which was constructed in 1975; even this requires constant maintenance.

Bay Town's architecture, substantially unchanged since the 18th and 19th centuries when the community became a successful fishing and merchandise port, vividly reflects the past, though you must turn a blind eye to the inevitable shop and restaurant frontages that honeycomb the place. Red pantiled houses descend higgledy-piggledy from clifftop to seashore, linked by steep alleyways and narrow passages. It will come as no surprise that Robin Hood's Bay was something of a Mecca for smuggling; a well known claim from the days of Revenue men and contraband is that a bale of silk could be passed from one end of the village to the other without ever seeing daylight by the use of secret interconnecting doors and tunnels.

The Scarborough to Whitby railway came in 1885 and with it new markets for fish and the beginnings of tourism. Although the line closed in 1965, Bay Town has continued to attract visitors who arrive by road in ever greater numbers. Walkers on the Coast to Coast route pioneered by Alfred Wainwright traditionally dip a boot into the North Sea to celebrate completing their trek from the Irish Sea at St. Bees. They do so at The Dock, Bay Town's diminutive waterfront near the Bay Hotel. Lack of a proper harbour severely restricted the size of vessels able to work from here, a major factor in the village's commercial decline around the turn of the 20th century.

As well as historical and epicurean delights, Robin Hood's Bay is renowned for its stunning geology. At low tide there is access out to West Scar, Landing Scar and East Scar, a vast wave-cut platform of swirling ledges, the eroded remnants of a great dome of rock from the Middle Jurassic that once dominated the bay. The chaotic, slumped cliffs provide rich pickings for observant and skilled fossil-hunters, but care must be taken not to get cut off by the tide.

From the bottom of Bay Town, turn right up Albion Road. Where it swings right, watch for a wooden Cleveland Way wall sign on the left and climb the stone steps. Higher up, timber steps lead on to a clifftop boardwalk and you soon reach a kissing gate at a "Path Closed" sign. Go through the gate then turn left over a succession of three stiles through fields; this brings you to the deep steps at the National Trust's Boggle Hole.

Cross the footbridge with the youth hostel to your right, proceed left, then right at the lane. Almost immediately, steps on the left climb back to clifftop level with marvellous views opening up back to Bay Town and ahead to the Raven Hall Hotel. Follow the path and descend steps to the footbridge over Stoupe Beck near the beach. Here a paved but often muddy bridleway leads uphill past Stoupe Bank Farm, to a country lane. Just past the next farm, Stoupebrow Cottage, a waymark directs the trail back to the cliffline and you soon pass a World War II pillbox set in a commanding position on Peter White Cliff.

About 800m/yds further on, at a "National Trust Ravenscar" sign, ignore the track on the right and continue along the path, crossing over two timber bridges to join a track. Pass a house access track and a sign indicating the old alum works. The trail now climbs steadily on a waymarked track to the right up through low, scrubby woods past the overgrown waste shale of the Ravenscar Alum Works.

Particularly during the 18th and 19th centuries, the seaward flank of Brow Moor was extensively quarried for alum. With a history dating back to 1600, such workings are a common sight along the Cleveland Way: locations already passed include Carlton Bank on the Cleveland Hills, Boulby and Sandsend. Producing alum was a labour intensive and time-consuming business. The shale was fired with brushwood, mixed with water, concentrated by boiling and mixed with an alkali – usually urine shipped here by the barrel-load from London's pubs! Alum crystals formed when the solution cooled, but this complex method of production ended when a cheaper alternative source was discovered using colliery waste. Ravenscar's alum quarry closed down in 1862; fifty years later it became the site of a brickworks whose kilns and railway sidings, though largely disintegrated, are still discernible.

Take the left fork ahead and at the second Y-junction fork left again on to a brick-laid trackway only a stone's throw from the disused Whitby to Scarborough railway line.

Engineered by John Waddell, the railway was operational from 1885 to 1965, when the infamous Dr. Beeching axed many of Britain's branch lines. Running midway between sea and moor and served by eight stations, the 21-mile (34km) line was one of the most spectacular in the country. From Bay Town to Ravenscar the gradient, though imperceptible to walkers, is considerable, accounting for a 431ft (131m) height gain in 5 miles (8km). The clifftop tunnel was built to by-pass Raven Hall, home then of a railway director. Today, here and there, subsidence interrupts the trackbed, graphically illustrating the area's geological instability. In Nature's way, wildflowers and shrubs have colonised the banks, including broom, whose black seed pods crack open audibly on warm summer days.

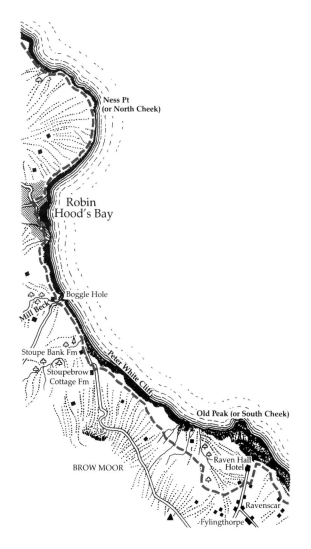

Ness Pt
(or North Cheek)

Robin
Hood's Bay

Boggle Hole

Mill Beck

Stoupe Bank Fm

Peter White Cliff

Stoupebrow
Cottage Fm

Old Peak (or South Cheek)

BROW MOOR

Raven Hall
Hotel

Ravenscar

Fylingthorpe

A short distance ahead up the brick track, a concrete path is reached leading to the National Trust's Coastal Centre at Ravenscar.

The Trust owns the old overgrown alum quarries as well as a dramatic section of cliffs around Old Peak, or South Cheek. Walkers wishing to explore the quarries or the cliffs and shoreline can follow a waymarked Geological Trail with the help of an explanatory booklet available at the Information Centre. South Cheek headland is protected by a prominent reef of resistant Middle Lias rock associated with the great Peak Fault which runs seaward as a well-defined edge. Down at beach level, the skeletons of small creatures are preserved as fossils, notably ammonites, oysters and belemnites, while many of the pebbles and boulders are erratics, carried here by receding glaciers during the last Ice Age.

Right on the clifftop stands the imposing, castellated Raven Hall, now a hotel. It was built in 1774 on the site of a Roman Signal Station at 600ft (183m) above the sea. George III was treated here for madness, that most imprecise of terms, before finally succumbing in 1811. Subsequently the hall and gardens were extended by the Willis family and the hotel now boasts magnificent gardens, a golf course and open-air swimming pool, all open to non-residents. Perhaps of more immediate interest to Cleveland Wayfarers will be the bar which welcomes walkers. Ravenscar is the eastern terminus of the 40-mile (64km) Lyke Wake Walk whose start near Osmotherley was also passed by the Cleveland Way.

Pass the hotel entrance and walk along Station Road for about 100m/yds where a track on the left leads back to the cliffline.

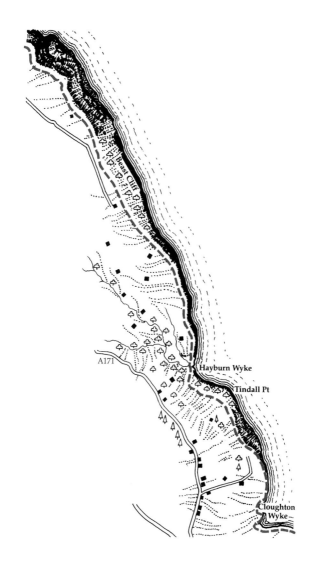

Beast Cliff

A171

Hayburn Wyke

Tindall Pt

Cloughton Wyke

Before leaving Ravenscar, spare a thought for what might have been. In the 1890s, ambitious plans were laid to develop the hamlet into a new holiday resort that would rival Scarborough. Over the ensuing 20 years, with the railway already in place, plots of land were sold, sewers installed, roadways laid out. A few villas did get built, but the hoped-for boom never materialised and the development company eventually went bankrupt. No doubt Ravenscar's location was just too exposed and inhospitable for prospective investors.

Following the high level coast path past a coastguard lookout, the rugged cliffs of South Peak soften as you approach Beast Cliff. Bushes, bracken and even small trees colonise a lower shelf (a Site of Special Scientific Interest), while inland the scenery is richly pastoral.

The trail continues straightforwardly, dipping gently with views far ahead to Scarborough Castle and Filey Brigg, where the Cleveland Way ends. From a stile drop steeply down steps into the wooded valley of Hayburn Wyke (small inlets or bays on the Yorkshire coast are called 'wyke'). At the footbridge spanning Hayburn Beck, a short detour left leads to a rocky platform above a little waterfall where an easy scramble leads to a wild beach of ankle-twisting pebbles and boulders.

Public access to the lovely deciduous woodland here is unrestricted, but the Yorkshire Naturalists' Trust who manage this nature reserve ask visitors not to pick flowers or otherwise damage the fragile environment.

As the Way now tackles the far uphill slope, the

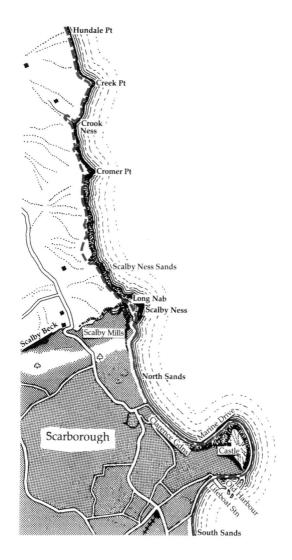

Hundale Pt

Creek Pt

Crook
Ness

Cromer Pt

Scalby Ness Sands

Long Nab

Scalby Ness

Scalby Beck

Scalby Mills

North Sands

Scarborough

Clarence Gdns

Marine Drive

Castle

Old Harbour

Lifeboat Stn

South Sands

pathside in late springtime is ablaze with bluebells, anemones and celandines. Fork left at both junctions ahead to emerge on the clifftop path alongside level fields above Tindall Point. Half an hour's walking will bring you to Cloughton Wyke, a haunt of sea anglers.

The words "Salt Pans" appear on the OS 1:25,000 map, referring no doubt to days when sea water was evaporated to produce salt, a vital preservative for fish catches before the advent of refrigeration.

Cloughton village and the main A171 Scarborough road lie just inland, but the Cleveland Way now jinks inland and back again at Cloughton Wyke before rounding precipitous Hundale Point. There are no difficulties ahead as the trail passes a coastguard lookout at Creek Point, takes the down-and-up steps through the Crook Ness ravine, cuts across Cromer Point above Sailor's Grave and reaches Scalby Ness at the northern threshold of Scarborough. (A path above Scalby Ness Sands leads to the coast road and youth hostel.)

Keep to seaward of Scalby Beck along the gorsey slopes of Long Nab; from this promontory the whole of North Bay sweeps into view. Steps lead down from the end of Long Nab to a footbridge over Scalby Beck where you turn left past the Sealife Centre. There a pedestrian promenade joins Royal Albert Drive towards the castle, flanked by Clarence Gardens.

Scarborough's name is thought to derive from the Old Norse "Scardeburg" – stronghold of Skarthi. Its twin bays are divided by the craggy bulk of a central headland, in turn an Iron Age fortification, Roman Signal Station, and site of a 12th-century Norman castle whose battlemented ruins crown the summit today.

The town has a commercial harbour and marina, but is perhaps best known for its fine bathing beaches and entertainments which have earned it pride of place among East Coast resorts. Indeed it was one of England's very first seaside resorts, having developed as a spa in the 17th century with the discovery of sulphurous springs said to possess healing properties.

When a local doctor set the trend for sea bathing, Scarborough's popularity increased still further, and it only needed the railway connection which came in 1845 to assure the town's prosperity. With characteristic Victorian enthusiasm and confidence, great hotels and promenades were built, theatres were opened, pleasure gardens landscaped. Holidaymakers flocked here to "take the waters" and indulge in traditional seaside activities which, technology apart, differ little from today's.

From Royal Albert Drive above North Sands, follow Marine Drive around the castle headland. (It was begun in 1897, but the first contractor went bankrupt and the toll drive was not opened until 1908. Three years earlier the North Promenade pier had been wrecked during a January storm.)

After the old tollhouse adjacent to East Pier, flank the marina and harbour, pass the lifeboat station and continue along Foreshore Road above South Sands to the spa. Scarborough's original claim to fame, the spa is now used as an entertainments

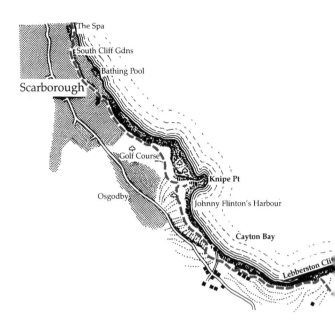

Scarborough

The Spa
South Cliff Gdns
Bathing Pool

Golf Course
Knipe Pt
Osgodby
Johnny Flinton's Harbour
Cayton Bay
Lebberston Cli

and conference centre; the cafe may be of interest
to walkers.

Climb steps on the right and follow the main path
to the left which zigzags uphill through a
complexity of flowery paths to reach the clifftop
Esplanade. Turn left past South Cliff Gardens on
the broad pathway under a clock tower and
through the end of Holbeck Gardens.

Take the waymarked path on the left through trees
then on along the top of Wheatcroft Cliff and
White Nab, flanking the golf course. Continuing

straight ahead down and up steps, the trail then joins a path on the left above wooded hillside.

Beyond a gate where a path joins from the right at the edge of Osgodby's housing, bear left towards the wooded undercliff of Knipe Point, owned by the National Trust.

Steps lead down to a waymarked track on the right and in 100m/yds take a path on the right down more steps. After a further 150m/yds bear right again. You soon pass an access path to Johnny Flinton's Harbour, but carry on ahead, taking the waymarked fork left nearby wind-sculpted trees.

Above Cayton Sands the trail continues to a stile then climbs a steep bank on the right. At the top bear left across the field and down to the access lane for the Cayton Sands cafe and toilets. Cross the lane and follow the downward path opposite, soon passing another beach access path on Killerby Cliff.

There now ensues straightforward clifftop walking round precipitous Red Cliff Point and on above narrow Gristhorpe Sands, the inland scene dominated for a while by caravans and holiday park development. From Cunstone Nab, journey's end is in prospect, a mere hour or so's walking away.

Before local government reorganisation in 1974, the Cleveland Way officially ended atop Newbiggin Cliff, the boundary between the East Riding of Yorkshire and the North Riding, under whose auspices the trail was originally designated. With administrative responsibility now shared by North Yorkshire County Council and

Redcar and Cleveland Borough Council, the Way term-inates more sensibly at Filey.

First, however, follow the cliff path along the headland (Carr Naze) and out on to Filey Brigg. If tide and sea conditions are favourable you can descend to the rocky foreshore and savour this elemental spot at the easternmost extremity of the trail. Afterwards either walk along the beach to Coble Landing if the tide is low, or return to West Cliff Country Park on the headland where a popular path makes a beeline for Filey's seafront.

Set back from the sea on a steep slope with wonderful sea views, Filey's ranks of Victorian terraced houses overlook

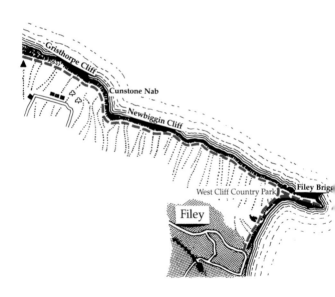

a huge sweep of sheltered sandy beach stretching southwards for some 6 miles (9.5km). Despite its modern holiday attractions, the town's origins as a fishing village are still in evidence, nowhere more vividly than at the northern end of the promenade where colourful fishing cobles are hauled up by tractor on to hard standing.

4   Reverse directions

From Filey's seafront set off north past Coble Landing to West Cliff Country Park, making a detour out on to Filey Brigg if desired. Veering north-west at Carr Naze headland, the trail continues along North and Newbiggin cliffs, round Cunstone Nab and along the seaward perimeter of caravan and holiday parks above Gristhorpe Sands. Once round Red Cliff Point near Lebberston you pass above Cayton Sands, crossing the cafe access lane into a field.

In 200m/yds turn right steeply downhill then left along the undercliff path. Cross the pathway to Johnny Flinton's Harbour and continue ahead, joined by a path from the right. Two sets of uphill steps follow in quick succession, the trail keeping left at junctions here in the wooded undercliff of Knipe Point. You emerge past a path to Osgodby where straightforward clifftop progress is resumed.

Rounding White Nab the Way approaches Scarborough along Wheatcroft Cliff flanking the golf course. Beyond a car park you reach a surfaced path and a descent through a small ravine, emerging at the southern end of Holbeck Gardens.

Walk past the clocktower along the broad walkway beside South Cliff Gardens, turning right off the Esplanade down a zigzagging path then right again down steps to The Spa. (Many pleasant alternative routes exist downhill through Holbeck and South Cliff gardens, reaching either South Bay bathing pool or The Spa.)

Continue north along the seafront to meet Foreshore Road above South Sands. Passing the lifeboat station and harbour you will enter Marine Drive taking you round the castle headland and joining Royal Albert Drive above North Sands. The pedestrian promenade passes a Sealife Centre, beyond which you cross the Scalby Beck footbridge and climb steps on the right up on to Long Nab.

The trail now heads north along the seaward edge of farmland, cuts across Cromer Point and takes the down-and-up steps through Crook Ness ravine. Passing a coastguard lookout at Creek Point, you round precipitous Hundale Point and detour inland a short distance to negotiate Cloughton Wyke.

Straightforward clifftop walking follows round Tindall Point. Little Cliff is wooded and the Way turns down right through the trees, keeping right again further down to reach a footbridge over Hayburn Beck, with Hayburn Wyke waterfall just along at the seashore.

Steep steps climb north from the valley to a stile where the clifftop path resumes, gently gaining height above sprawling Beast Cliff. About a mile (1.6 km) past a coastguard lookout, a track on the left leads inland to Station Road at Ravenscar. Turn right and cross the road in front of the Raven Hall Hotel entrance, to a National Trust information centre and a descending brick-laid track. Keep right at two Y-junctions further on, descending scrubby hillside then bearing left on a track. The trail continues past a house access and crosses two timber bridges.

Leaving the National Trust's Ravenscar property, a cross-field course returns you to the cliffline. Beyond a wartime pillbox on Peter White Cliff, bear left to join a country lane, turning right past Stoupebrow Cottage Farm and Stoupe Bank Farm. From here a paved bridleway descends to a footbridge over Stoupe Beck near beach level.

Steps lead out to the clifftop and in 500m/yds more steps take you down to a lane near Boggle Hole Youth Hostel. Turn right then almost immediately left to the footbridge (hostel on your left), climb the steep steps then take the field path over three stiles to a kissing gate at a "Path Closed" sign.

The trail now follows a clifftop boardwalk, descends timber steps then stone steps leading into Albion Road. From the bottom of Robin Hood's Bay, ascend the road to the top car park and continue along Station Road (B1477), turning right at a waymark post.

Walk along Mount Pleasant North and into a grassy track past houses. Through undergrowth, a kissing gate gives access to the onward cliff path which sweeps round North Cheek headland past a coastguard lookout.

Apart from steeper gradients at Rain Dale and

above Maw Wyke Hole, the going is straightforward along the clifftops all the way to the slopes of Ling Hill. Here you drop to the access lane behind Whitby lighthouse, immediately crossing a wall stile on the right and angling back down to the cliffline path which soon passes the Fog Signal buildings.

A succession of field-edge stiles leads on to Saltwick Bay Holiday Park. Walk ahead past the shop and camping grounds on the surfaced lane, curving right then left behind Saltwick Nab promontory. A surfaced path now makes a beeline for Whitby's East Cliff television mast and coast-guard station. Bear left to reach St. Mary's Church and the top of Church Stairs' 199 steps. Whitby Abbey is passed to your left.

At the bottom of the steps go left along Church Street, turn right and cross Whitby's swing bridge over the River Esk, with the town centre ahead. The Way continues along the quayside past the fish market and out towards West Pier. If the tide is low you can beach-walk right along to Sandsend. Otherwise, turn left up past the whalebone arch and Captain Cook's statue and take the clifftop path heading west above Whitby Sands.

The path, forced inland at a ravine spanned by a footbridge, skirts the golf course and reaches the main A174 road opposite a caravan park. Turn right and follow the roadside past the golf course, through Upgang Chine and along the shoreline to East Row village. The road jinks inland to cross East Row Beck and soon arrives at Sandsend.

From the car park adjacent to Sandsend Beck where the road heads inland, climb the flights of steps on to the old Loftus to Whitby railway trackbed. This takes you out past the overgrown Ness End and Deep Grove alum quarries to a sealed tunnel portal.

Here at Deepgrove Wyke, steep steps then a sharp right turn lead to a gently undulating path above eroded cliffs, further on shadowing the railway trackbed around Kettleness Point. Veering left the Way reaches Kettleness hamlet, turns right at the road-end to pass through Kettleness Farm, and soon resumes its cliffline course outside fields.

Arriving at High Cliff, the railway trackbed sweeps inland round the deep valley of Calais Beck, but the Cleveland Way descends steps right down to sea level, crossing a stream at the bottom, near caves known as Hob Holes. A beach-walk along the sands past the Sailing Club brings you to Runswick Bay.

The beach slipway takes you to the bottom of the village where a stepped path weaves up between the cottages to meet the old road (now a track). Turn up right and join Bank Top Lane along to the road junction at the Runswick Bay Hotel. Turn right and follow the fenced path seaward to a stile, then bearing left along the cliff path. Beyond the little waterfall above Rosedale Wyke, the trail reaches the road at Port Mulgrave.

Bear right, walk past the old coastguard cottages and continue over the shoulder of Beacon Hill, eventually descending pasture to a stiled field path some way back from the cliff edge. Just past some farm buildings the Way drops down a groove then steps into Church Street at Staithes.

Walk down past Captain Cook's Cottage and turn left round past the seafront Cod & Lobster Inn, continuing along the cobbled main street to a short lane on the right leading to the footbridge over Staithes Beck. Once across the beck, turn left and climb steeply up Cowbar Lane, following it westwards until, at a left bend, the trail forks off right over fields to Boulby.

Keeping seaward of the houses, you next tackle the ascent on to rugged Boulby Cliff, highest on the English eastern seaboard. In 1¼ miles (2km) the Way slants downhill as a stiled field path, passes Warren Cottage and turns right to the cliffline at Snilah Pond above Hummersea Scar. Gradually at first then more steeply, you drop into the Kilton Beck valley at Skinningrove, crossing the road bridge and bearing right along Marine Terrace.

Bear right from the car park, taking the switchback path to the jetty underpass then a stretch through the dunes behind Cattersty Sands. Steps lead up from the beach to a steep climb on to the clifftop where the trail turns right along the edge of pasture and fields.

For about 500 m/yds the mineral railway line from Boulby potash mine is followed round the flanks of Warsett Hill, then you are on Hunt Cliff and approaching Old Saltburn. A gentle descent gives way to stepped hillside bringing you down to the Ship Inn.

Follow the main A174 over Skelton Beck and turn left up the road hairpins (short cut by steps). About 100m/yds beyond Saltburn's railway station access road, branch left and in 250m/yds left again down a path above Valley Gardens. (Alternatively you could walk through the gardens from the seafront.)

Ignoring side paths, the level woodland trail ends at a lane by a seat; here you turn left downhill, joining an enclosed pathway coming in from Marske Mill on the left. Pass beneath the railway viaduct and cross Skelton Beck footbridge.

The Way now continues upstream, soon doubling back and climbing quite steeply up through Crow Wood. You emerge on a clear path over fields (possible further residential development in future), and walk up Derwent Road.

Turn right into Ullswater Road then left up Coniston Road to the main A173 at Skelton. Take the steps directly opposite, turn right along a lane for 100m/yds at The Hills then turn left on a field path which becomes surfaced and reaches the main Boosbeck Road at Skelton Green.

Walk straight ahead up Airy Hill Lane which beyond Airy Hill Farm becomes a field track then a path curving right along field edges to a stile above Rawcliff Banks Wood. Follow the fenced path left to the top of a quarry whose east rim is descended on steps through gorse to a stile. Track and path lead out to the end of terraced houses where a left turn following the old by-passed road will bring you round past the Fox and Hounds pub at Slapewath.

Cross the bridge and the busy A171 and walk east along the old road to a stile and track on the right. Doubling back west now, the trail gains height, forking right on to a level path. Ahead, cross a metal stile and pass a clearing in the woods, watching for a stile on the left where the Way drops through Spa Wood.

It passes another clearing and descends inside the edge of the trees to a narrow fenced path. At the end, turn left up the farm driveway, leaving it further on by a stile on the right. Cross the field and streambed to reach a handgate and join a track heading south-west outside Guisborough Woods. (NOTE: follow map and directions carefully over the next section).

A left bend takes you up into the woods where you turn right at a junction on to a predominantly level stretch of walking. Almost a mile (1,500m) later you pass a track on the left and then after a short downhill right-hand bend leave the track for a path on the right which climbs gently to the broad, scarp-edge forestry road. Highcliff Nab is off to the right of this. From it, turn south, steeply downhill, cross a forestry track, bear left at a cleared area and right at a handgate to conclude the forestry section.

Walk along outside Highcliffe Farm's fields, cross the little valley of The Race and climb over the moorland of Black Nab to meet the medieval road across the moors from Guisborough Priory to Kirkbymoorside. Turn right then in 200m/yds left along the edge of Hutton Lowcross Woods to a gated corner. Here the Way heads west over heathery Newton Moor to a gate.

The out-and-back detour to climb Roseberry Topping is straightforward on a clear path, though in wind or mist care is needed around the precipitous summit, ravaged by landslip and quarrying.

Back at the gate on Newton Moor the trail resumes in a south-easterly direction above Slacks Wood, swinging south beside a wall on the lip of Great Ayton Moor and dropping steeply to Gribdale Gate, a popular picnic area at the lane-end above Great Ayton. Continue straight ahead up a broad stony track between trees, with steps finally leading out on to Easby Moor. Head east from Captain Cook's Monument into the forestry on Coate Moor, joining a wide forest track and ignoring side turnings.

Further east at Pale End Plantation there is a sharp right turn downhill and out past Bankside Farm. Follow the country road down, over the infant River Leven and under the Esk Valley railway line. At the junction ahead, a left turn leads to the Esk Valley road at Kildale.

Walk south-west from the village along the road for 500m/yds then turn up left towards the moors. Climbing the edge of Warren Moor, the lane gains height steadily, drops slightly from a cattle grid and reaches an acute left bend leading down to Baysdale Farm. Here the Cleveland Way continues straight on along a stony track over Battersby Moor, gradually climbing round Tidy Brown Hill and meeting the Cleveland Hills escarpment.

Further along at Greenhow Bank the trail rises a little, curves past Burton Howe tumuli and passes the remains of a 19th-century moorland cross. The Way continues south-east along the old coaching road to Bloworth Crossing, site of a level crossing where the road was bisected by the Rosedale Ironstone Railway. Here turn sharp right, following the well-defined route of an old pannierway up to Cockayne Head and on to Botton Head (or Round Hill), highest point on the North York Moors at 1,490ft (454m).

Trending north-west, the trail descends over Urra Moor which narrows to Carr Ridge and from whose peaty crest the path drops near to a rocky groove. Lower down, grassy hillsides lead to a gate and the B1257 road at Clay Bank Top. (From here a bad weather alternative on old jet mining tracks skirts the escarpment along to just beyond Cringle Moor.)

A hefty ascent now follows, partly stepped, up on to Hasty Bank – first in a succession of big down-and-ups along the Cleveland Hills escarpment. An exciting path down through The Wainstones leads to Garfit Gap and the ensuing climb on to Cold Moor. The clear pitched path then drops through another col before attacking the slopes of Cringle Moor. In a broad sweep above the precipitous crags of Kirby Bank, the trail reaches the Alex Falconer memorial toposcope on Cringle End, then drops as a broad track over rough pasture towards the cafe and road at Carlton Bank.

Across the road you ascend through old alum workings to emerge at the summit of Carlton Moor. Continuing along the escarpment, past the gliding club airfield, leads round Gold Hill and Live Moor. Descending gradually at first, then steeply down steps through Live Moor Plantation, the Way turns left along a track outside the lower wood, swinging right past overgrown mine spoil to a telephone box at Huthwaite Green crossroads.

Cross over and walk down past Hollin Hill Farm, over the Scugdale Beck road bridge and a ford. Climbing to the top of a pasture field, the onward Way bears right on a broad pathway threading along the lower edge of Coalmire Plantation for about 800m/yds. Following a sharp left turn, you gain height quite rapidly before contouring through the forest to a gate and cattle grid at the Scarth Nick road.

Almost opposite on the right, the trail continues as a well-worn path across the open flanks of Scarth Wood Moor, approaching the upper edge of Arncliff Wood at a gate. Beyond the trig pillar on Beacon Hill and a BT booster station, follow the cart track downhill through South Wood and out across fields past Chapel Wood Farm (access to Mount Grace Priory and Lady Chapel).

This swings east into Rueberry Lane and meets the

Swainby road just north of Osmotherley. Turn right and walk down to the village's market cross.

Directly over on the left at the crossroads, a waymarked archway marks the trail's continuation past the old Methodist chapel, along a short flag path, over Back Lane and out across two fields. Steps lead down through trees to a footbridge over Cod Beck and once out of the woods you keep to the left of White House Farm to reach a stile. Turn right along Green Lane and at the Osmotherley-Hawnby road cross over and take the next turning right (south-east).

Over a couple of fields the Way drops through woods, crosses a bridge at the lower reservoir, and passes the former Oak Dale Farm. Walk up Oak Dale along the north shore of the upper reservoir to a shady copse and Jenny Brewster's Spring. The route now climbs the steepish, brackeny slopes of Thimbleby Moor to meet the Osmotherley to Hawnby road again at a bend.

Heading due south the trail joins the course of the ancient Hambleton Drove Road, climbing past the edge of moorside forestry and up on to Black Hambleton whose summit lies a short distance off route. The broad stony trackway snakes over the moortop for more than a mile then makes a pronounced right turn (due south again) at White Gill Head. Enclosed between walls for a while, the Drove Road reaches a gate then crosses the old road from Kepwick to Hawnby.

Still flanked by a wall, continue south, gradually

swinging south-east over Little Moor to Steeple Cross at a corner of Boltby Forest. For just over 800m/yds the trail lies inside the forest, emerging at a gate and continuing its south-easterly direction.

Soon a right turn takes you off the drove road and past High Paradise Farm. Walk down the access lane, bearing left through hillside trees and passing above Low Paradise Farm. This forestry track reaches the road at Sneck Yate Bank where you cross over and walk uphill to a gate, the path now following the Hambleton Hills escarpment. Beyond High Barn the trail skirts a disused quarry, passes an Iron Age hill fort and continues alongside arable farmland above South Woods.

A corner in the scarp brings you above dramatic Whitestone Cliff. Gormire Lake lies below, cradled in Garbutt Wood which is reached by a nature trail path on the right a little further ahead. The Way soon reaches the A170 road at Sutton Bank. Nearby are a car park, picnic area, toilets and a National Park Information Centre with cafe.

About 500m/yds ahead along the escarpment path, a left turn into Kilburn Moor Plantation beside the Castern Dike earthwork takes the Cleveland Way east towards Helmsley. But first there is an official out-and-back detour to Kilburn White Horse (allow an hour). Simply follow the southbound scarp edge path past the gliding club airfield, swinging round above the cliffs of Roulston Scar and reaching a point above the White Horse.

Steps are now retraced to Castern Dike which leads

out to the A170 at a junction with the Kilburn road. Cross over and pass the Hambleton Hotel, taking a left turn just beyond down a surfaced driveway towards Hambleton House. Bear right, staying south of the stables and picking up a rough forestry track at the plantation's edge. The Way soon veers left across fields as Cote Moor Road, a rutted track which becomes surfaced and enters the western end of Cold Kirby.

Walk through the village, swinging right past the church and up into Low Field Lane, a straight track over the fields ending in a little overgrown valley which descends to Flassen Dale. Turn left on the track to Grass Keld Spring and bear right to reach a gateway at the junction ahead.

The trail crosses the stream and leads into Bridge Road, another forestry track. Passing small lakes in Nettle Dale you eventually meet the country road from Scawton, turning left and walking along to Rievaulx Bridge over the River Rye. (Rievaulx Abbey ruins stand just over 900m/yds to the left and if time allows are well worth exploring.)

Cross the bridge and stay on the road for about 800m/yds until it curves left up Ingdale Howl. Here the trail branches right, uphill through Quarry Bank and Whinny Bank woods. At the top it passes Griff Lodge, crosses the access track and takes steps down and up through the little Blackdale Howl Wood valley.

Turn right at the top and walk along field head-lands above the woods, striking up left to a gate, then turning right to join a walled farm track heading directly towards Helmsley with good views of the castle. Entering the town along appropriately-named Cleveland Way, you pass the church lychgate entrance and arrive at Helmsley's market cross, the trail's terminus.

5 The Tabular Hills Link

Those walkers wishing to convert the Cleveland Way into a circular route can do so by following the 48 mile (77km) Tabular Hills Link, adding approximately four days to the overall trek. This Regional Route is an initiative of the North York Moors National Park Authority and is supported by the Countryside Commission, English Tourist Board, Rural Development Commission, Yorkshire and Humberside Tourist Board, Ryedale District Council and Scarborough Borough Council. Comprehensive background detail and maps for the link are contained in a booklet published by the North York Moors National Park.

As well as the convenience of returning to the start point (particularly if a vehicle has been parked), this link along the southern boundary of the North York Moors National Park provides fascinating scenic contrasts. The Tabular Hills rise gently from the south to between 500ft (150m) and 1,000ft (300m), culminating in north-facing 'nabs' or scarps. Where the underlying geology is limestone, wildflowers abound with the land laid down to arable crops and grass. Elsewhere on the less fertile Calcareous Grits lie dramatic swathes of conifer forest, while narrow dales cutting south into the moors contain ancient woodlands.

The route itself connects Helmsley with the coast at Scalby Ness Sands just north of Scarborough. Along the way it passes through a series of picturesque villages on the escarpment edge before sampling moors and forests with fewer amenities. Waymarking is by signpost and a special 'link' logo on the familiar yellow and blue arrows denoting footpaths and bridleways respectively.

Before embarking on this return link to Helmsley, purists will wish to complete the Cleveland Way's final leg. This entails walking the 11-mile (18km) stretch from Scarborough to Filey, then simply catching a bus or train back to Scarborough.

To begin the Tabular Hills Link, retrace your steps along the Cleveland Way north to Scalby Mills, cross the footbridge and traverse the flank of Long Nab to the clifftop path above Scalby Ness Sands. In about 300m/yds the Tabular Hills Link sets off south-west along the edge of fields to a stile and the Burniston Road. Turn right, then in a short distance, left along Station Road, Scalby. In the town centre bear left along Scalby Road, and on meeting Scalby Beck turn right parallel to it, crossing the road ahead at a double-arched bridge. Swinging west, walk along the bank of Sea Cut to Mowthorpe Bridge.

Sea Cut, built some two centuries ago by local engineer Sir George Cayley, takes excess floodwater surges from the River Derwent and channels them to the sea at Scalby Ness – actually the river's original course before North Sea ice diverted it south during the last Ice Age.

Before the drain's construction, the Vale of Pickering was subject to serious flooding.

Cross Mowthorpe Bridge and follow the road past Mowthorpe Farm, up past Everley, noting to your left the start of Sea Cut at Weir Head.

Take a sharp left turn to Wrench Green and once over the river bridge bear left then right, passing cottages on your right. Soon the road becomes a forest track (Lang Gate) leading to a cross junction. Bear right here then follow the waymarked track due west through Wykeham Forest.

Here in one of Forest Enterprise's commercial woodlands Sitka spruce is king, but Douglas fir, Scots pine and larch also grow, with some pockets of broad-leaved trees providing more diverse wildlife habitats.

Carry straight on past the trig pillar at Highwood Brow and follow the forestry road curving south-west past the large tree nursery to a gated exit. The track continues to a country road near Cockmoor Hall which the trail crosses near a popular picnic area. Walk in the same direction through a wooded section and along to another road, bearing right past Givendale Head Farm, and back into forestry.

Prehistoric multiple dykes, such as nearby Cockmoor and Oxmoor, have survived largely because the afforested land has not been ploughed up for cultivation.

Keep right at the junction ahead and follow the unsurfaced road along the edge of Dalby Forest, joining the Forest Drive. Branch off left about

300m/yds beyond a car park on to another unsurfaced road (New Road) which swings north-west through forest to the Crosscliff viewpoint.

Although Dalby Forest is now concerned mainly with commercial conifer production, this area is steeped in history, from ancient burial mounds called 'howes' to remnants of the once great herds of deer hunted by kings 600 years ago in a royal forest that stretched from Pickering to Scarborough.

Eventually the trail emerges from forest on to Newgate Moor. It joins the access lane to Newgate Foot Farm and continues north-west as "Old Wife's Way", part of an old packhorse route between Malton and Robin Hood's Bay. Through a small plantation you reach the A169 at Saltergate Brow.

Two conspicuous landmarks have been in view to the north: the smooth, heathery summit of Blakey Topping, and the extraordinary pyramid of the MOD's Fylingdales Early Warning Station, replacing the old "golf ball" structures.

A narrow path descends beside the road to the hairpin bend where the Tabular Hills Link turns off left at a gate and stile into the Hole of Horcum. Instead of dropping into this vast depression, however, it keeps ahead round the western moorland rim past Seavy Pond and the heads of several "griffs", or side-valleys.

The Hole of Horcum is a natural hollow excavated, along with neighbouring Newton Dale, by water escaping from the ice-dammed lake which filled Eskdale some 10,000 years ago towards the end of the last Ice Age. Legend has attributed its formation to a local giant, Wade, who is reputed to have scooped up a gargantuan fistful of earth which he threw in a fit of anger as far as he could; it became Blakey Topping!

Reaching Dundale Pond, continue south up Limpsey Gate Lane to Levisham village, passing the Horseshoe Inn.

Although somewhat isolated, Levisham thrives as a pleasant, timeless place with broad grassy verges backed by picturesque cottages and farmhouses.

Walk through the village and down the road's hairpin bend. At the bottom bear right into Hagg Wood Marsh Nature Reserve, at first not far from Levisham's curiously sited 11th-century church. Soon the trail crosses a stream and reaches the railway line at Farwath.

The Newton Dale gorge runs from the head of the Murk Esk valley to the Vale of Pickering and was chosen by George Stephenson for the course of his Pickering to Whitby railway line, opened in 1836. Closed by Beeching in 1964, the line from Grosmont to Pickering has since been resurrected by an independent trust to become one of the country's best-loved and most scenic steam railways.

The link route now heads north-west up wooded hillside (Farwath Road), passes Howlgate Farm and East Brow House and arrives at Newton-upon-Rawcliffe. Reaching the road, turn sharp right, descending Newton Bank and following the onward path into woods, over Raygate Slack and out across Stony Moor. Approaching forestry ahead, turn left along the edge of fields to a road opposite Taylor Hill Farm. Here turn left for about 200m/yds where the trail heads off right (west) as a lane (Peat Road). At the far end turn left down by the wood's edge then bear half right past Elleron Lodge over fields. You now enter woodland and cross a stream footbridge, swinging acutely right on a bridleway to Keldy Banks Farm and a road. Turn left, uphill to a T-junction where the way once again heads west, passing a turning to Cawthorne.

Cawthorne's Roman encampment, along with the splendid remains of a Roman road on Wheeldale Moor, Wade's Causeway, remind us of that momentous invasion by a foreign army back in the 1st century AD.

The arrow-straight road (High Lane) ends north of Cropton village where a short detour to the right will provide wonderful views over the adjacent moors and Tabular Hills. Just beyond Sycamore Farm walk right along a narrow pathway past St. Gregory's church and bear right down the road hill. Near the bottom turn left into a track trending south above Cropton Beck.

The trail bears right over the beck bridge and left to Appleton Mill Farm, before climbing to meet Hamley Lane. Turn left at the end, but instead of entering Appleton-le-Moors village, take a right turn into a track (South Ings Lane). At the gated cross-junction ahead, go right with Ings Balk path then left into Lingmoor Lane track.

The Tabular Hills Link now jinks north through

woods, up into Bottomfields Lane and on to a path between fields. Down the hill lies the much-visited village of Hutton-le-Hole.

A settlement since long before the days of recorded history, Hutton-le-Hole lies in a hollow between two limestone headlands. Its strong tradition of rural crafts, along with industries such as lime-burning, coal and ironstone mining have left a rich legacy for us modern-day sightseers to ponder. Centre stage is the Ryedale Folk Museum, opened in 1964 and packed with local exhibits reflecting daily life down through the centuries.

Walk through the village, forking left along Keld Lane. At a gate on the left turn off on to a waymarked field path which curves gradually west as a wide track. An intricacy of footbridges and small fields past Grouse Hall and behind the old mill leads up to Gillamoor church. Walk straight through the village and on to Fadmoor.

First turn left along Onams Lane then almost immediately turn right and right again on Green Lane. At the end bear left down Caldron Mill Road along field edges and follow the path which curves right then left down through woods to Hold Caldron Mill, once a busy corn-grinding centre. Cross the bridge and climb the path by a fence, turning sharp right at the top near a telegraph pole.

Continue beside the wood's perimeter for four fields then walk left to reach the Skiplam Road, turning right along tarmac past Skiplam Grange.

In about a mile (1.6km) bear left on a lane past

Nawton Tower and continue straight down the path ahead. Once over the track (Howldale Lane), the trail climbs through one belt of woodland, over and down to another. Angling up right and through a field boundary gate you reach Northfield Lane. Take the path opposite and descend the track sharp right, bringing you down to a T-junction.

Turn left and walk down past Hasty Bank farmhouse, cross the footbridge over the River Riccal and ascend the wooded western slopes of Riccal Dale, ending in a steep and narrow path leading out into fields at the wood's edge. Maintaining the same direction the way reaches a country road and turns left towards Carlton, with Helmsley now only a stone's throw to the south.

North of Carlton village bear right along the Keld Lane track which drops into the head of Ash Dale and doubles back left (south). The walk down Ash Dale is straightforward in a delightful wooded setting. A stile on the right leads into the final stretch of waymarked field path zigzagging towards the rooftops of Helmsley which is entered via Warwick Place and Canons Garth Lane. Journey's end at Helmsley's market cross, where the Cleveland Way begins, completes a full circle of immensely varied and enjoyable walking.

Useful addresses

Cleveland Way Project Officer: North York Moors National Park, The Old Vicarage, Bondgate, Helmsley, York YO6 5BP. Tel (01439) 770657

Heritage Coast Ranger: The Moors Centre, Danby, Whitby, North Yorks. Tel (01287) 660540

Tourist Information Centres:

Helmsley – Market Place, Helmsley, York YO6 5DL. Tel (01439) 770173. Open daily April-October and winter weekends.

Sutton Bank – National Park Visitor Centre, Sutton Bank, Thirsk YO7 2EK. Tel (01845) 597426. Open daily April-October and winter weekends.

Great Ayton – High Green Car Park, Great Ayton, Cleveland TS9 6BJ. Tel (01642) 722835. Open Easter-October, weekdays and Sunday afternoons.

Guisborough – Priory Grounds, Church Street, Guisborough, Cleveland TS14 6HL. Tel (01287) 633801. Open daily but closed winter Mondays.

Saltburn – 4 Station Buildings, Saltburn, Cleveland TS12 1AQ. Tel (01287) 622422. Open Monday to Saturday, also Sundays during July and August.

Whitby – Langborne Road, Whitby YO21 1YN. Tel (01947) 602674. Open daily all year.

Ravenscar – National Trust Centre, Ravenscar, Scarborough. Tel (01723) 870138. Open daily end-March to end-September.

Scarborough – Unit 3, Valley Bridge Road, Scarborough YO11 1UZ. Tel (01723) 373333. Open daily all year.

Filey – John Street, Filey YO14 9DW.
Tel (01723) 512204. Open daily all year.

Camping & Caravanning Club of Great Britain, Greenfields House, Westwood Way, Coventry, West Midlands CV4 8JH

Countryside Commission, John Dower House, Crescent Place, Cheltenham, GL50 3RA

Forestry Commission, District Office, 42 Eastgate, Pickering, North Yorks.

National Trust, 36 Queen Anne's Gate, London, SW1H 9AS

Northumbria Tourist Board (for Cleveland), Aykley Heads, Durham, DH1 5UX

Ramblers' Association, 1/5 Wandsworth Road, London, SW8 2XX

Royal Society for the Protection of Birds, The Lodge, Sandy, Bedfordshire SG19 2DL

Youth Hostels' Association, Trevelyan House, St. Albans, Hertfordshire, AL1 2DY

Yorkshire and Humberside Tourist Board (for North Yorkshire), 312 Tadcaster Road, York, YO2 2HF

Acknowledgements

My thanks to Malcolm Hodgson, Cleveland Way Project Officer, and his colleagues for providing information and for kindly checking the accuracy of the route directions and maps. And to my daughter Fay and partner Stuart for their help on parts of the coastal section.

This book has been compiled in accordance with the Guidelines for Writers of Path Guides produced by the Outdoor Writers' Guild.

Dalesman Walking Guide Series

The Dalesman Walking Guide series is edited by Terry Marsh, one of the country's leading outdoor writers. Each edition is packed with detail given by experts with years of experience of walking the area. This series is aimed at the keen walker who is either familiar with the area or exploring a new walk, and who wants a reliable pocket sized guide with detailed colour maps showing the routes and main features.

NORTH PENNINES
Alan Hall 1-85568-105-6 165mm x 100mm 224 pages £7.99

WHITE PEAK
Martin Smith 1-85568-099-8 165mm x 100mm 224 pages £7.99

CLEVELAND WAY
Martin Collins 1-85568-113-7 165mm x 100mm 128 pages £6.99

SOUTH PENNINES
John Gillham 1-85568-106-4 165mm x 100mm 224 pages £7.99

DARK PEAK
John Gillham 1-85568-100-5 165mm x 100mm 192 pages £7.99

PENNINE WAY
Terry Marsh 1-85568-108-0 165mm x 100mm 192 pages £7.99

To accompany the series:

MOUNTAIN SAFETY

Kevin Walker 1-85568-112-9 165mm x 100mm 256 pages £8.99
A bible for all those who venture outdoors, be it camping, walking or climbing, with detailed advice on subjects ranging from choice of equipment to rope-work, survival and weather conditions, map reading and river crossings. Ideal for individuals as an essential guide for their own safety or as a reference book for group leaders wishing to give instruction on mountain safety.

Dalesman also publishes a successful pub walks series as well as books of shorter walks for families. If you wish to order any of the above books or would like a catalogue showing all Dalesman publications contact: Dalesman Publishing Co Ltd, FREEPOST LA1311, CLAPHAM, Lancaster, LA2 8BR (015242 51225).